APRIL
Monthly Idea Book

Ready-to-Use Templates, Activities, Management Tools, and More—for Every Day of the Month

Karen Sevaly

New York • Toronto • London • Auckland • Sydney
Mexico City • New Delhi • Hong Kong • Buenos Aires

Teaching *Resources*

DEDICATION

This book is dedicated to teachers and children everywhere.

Cover design by Maria Lilja
Cover art by Jillian Phillips
Interior design by Melinda Belter
Illustrations by Karen Sevaly

ISBN 978-0-545-37940-3

CONTENTS

FAVORITE TOPICS

CONTENTS

ENVIRONMENTAL AWARENESS

Reproducible Patterns

CHICKENS & EGGS

Reproducible Patterns

BUNNY RABBITS

Reproducible Patterns

APRIL SHOWERS

Reproducible Patterns

INCREDIBLE INSECTS

Reproducible Patterns

OLYMPIC GAMES

AWARDS, INCENTIVES, AND MORE

ANSWER KEY

INTRODUCTION

Welcome to the original Monthly Idea Book series! This book was written especially for teachers getting ready to teach topics related to the month of April.

Each book in this month-by-month series is filled with dozens of ideas for PreK–3 classrooms. Activities connect to the Common Core State Standards for Reading (Foundational Skills), among other subjects, to help you meet the needs of your students. (For more information, see page 16.)

Most everything you need to prepare the lessons and activities in this resource is included, such as:

- calendar and weather-related props

- book cover patterns and stationery for writing assignments

- booklet patterns

- games and puzzles that support learning in curriculum areas such as math, science, and writing

- activity sheets that help students organize information, respond to learning, and explore topics in a meaningful way

- patterns for projects that connect to holidays, special occasions, and commemorative events

All year long, you can weave the ideas and reproducible patterns in these unique books into your monthly lesson plans and classroom activities. Happy teaching!

What's Inside

You'll find that this book is chock-full of reproducibles that make lesson planning easier:

- puppets and picture props

- bookmarks, booklets, and book covers

- game boards, puzzles, and word finds

■ stationery

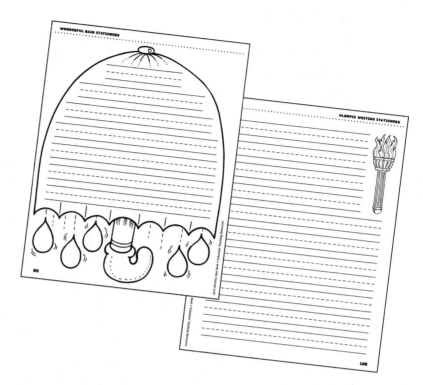

■ awards and certificates

How to Use This Book

The reproducible pages in this book have flexible use and may be modified to meet your particular classroom needs. Use the reproducible activity pages and patterns in conjunction with the suggested activities or weave them into your curriculum in other ways.

★ PHOTOCOPY OR SCAN

To get started, think about your developing lesson plans and upcoming bulletin boards. If desired, carefully remove the pages you will need. Duplicate those pages on copy paper, color paper, tagboard, or overhead transparency sheets. If you have access to a scanner, consider saving the pattern pages as PDF files. That way, you can size images up or down and customize them with text to create individualized lessons, center-time activities, interactive whiteboard lessons, homework pages, and more.

LAMINATE FOR DURABILITY

Laminating the reproducibles will help you extend their use. If you have access to a roll laminator, then you already know how fortunate you are when it comes to saving time and resources. If you don't have a laminator, clear adhesive vinyl covering works well. Just sandwich the pattern between two sheets of vinyl and cut off any excess. Then try some of these ideas:

- Put laminated sheets of stationery in a writing center to use for handwriting practice. Wipe-off markers work great on coated pages and can easily be erased with dry tissue.

- Add longevity to calendars, weather-related pictures, and pocket chart rebus pictures by preserving them with lamination.

- Transform picture props into flannel board figures. After lamination, add a tab of hook-and-loop fastener to the back of the props and invite students to adhere them to the flannel board for storytelling fun.

- To enliven magnet board activities, affix sections of magnet tape to the back of the picture props. Then encourage students to sort images according to the skills you're working on. For example, you might have them group images by commonalities such as initial sound, habitat, or physical attributes.

★ BULLETIN BOARDS

1. Set the Stage

Use background paper colors that complement many themes and seasons. For example, the dark background you used as a spooky display in October will have dramatic effect in November, when you begin a unit on woodland animals or Thanksgiving.

While paper works well, there are other background options available. You might also try fabric from a colorful bed sheet or gingham material. Discontinued rolls of patterned wallpaper can be purchased at discount stores. What's more, newspapers are easy to use and readily available. Attach a background of comics to set off a lesson on riddles, or use grocery store flyers to provide food for thought on a bulletin board about nutrition.

2. Make the Display

The reproducible patterns in this book can be enlarged to fit your needs. When we say enlarge, we mean it! Think BIG! Use an overhead projector to enlarge the images you need to make your bulletin board extraordinary.

If your school has a stencil press, you're lucky. The rest of us can use these strategies for making headers and titles.

- Cut strips of paper, cloud shapes, or cartoon bubbles. They will all look great! Then, by hand, write the text using wide-tipped permanent markers or tempera paint.

- If you must cut individual letters, use 4- by 6-inch pieces of construction paper. (Laminate first, if you can.) Cut the uppercase letters as shown on page 14. No need to measure, as somewhat irregular letters will look creative, not messy.

3. Add Color and Embellishments

Use your imagination! You'll be surprised at the great displays you can create.

- ■ Watercolor markers work great on small areas. On larger areas, you can switch to crayons, color chalk, or pastels. (Lamination will keep the color off of you. No laminator? A little hairspray will do the trick as a fixative.)

- ■ Cut character eyes and teeth from white paper and glue them in place. The features will really stand out and make your bulletin boards engaging.

- ■ For special effects, include items that provide texture and visual interest, such as buttons, yarn, and lace. Try cellophane or blue glitter glue on water scenes. Consider using metallic wrapping paper or aluminum foil to add a bit of shimmer to stars and belt buckles.

- ■ Finally, take a picture of your completed bulletin board. Store the photos in a recipe box or large sturdy envelope. Next year when you want to create the same display, you'll know right where everything goes. You might even want to supply students with pushpins and invite them to recreate the display, following your directions and using the photograph as support.

Staying Organized

Organizing materials with monthly file folders provides you with a location to save reproducible activity pages and patterns, along with related craft ideas, recipes, and magazine or periodical articles.

If you prefer, use file boxes instead of folders. You'll find that with boxes there will plenty of room to store enlarged patterns, sample art projects, bulletin board materials, and much more.

Meeting the Standards

CONNECTIONS TO THE COMMON CORE STATE STANDARDS

The Common Core State Standards Initiative (CCSSI) has outlined learning expectations in English/Language Arts, among other subject areas, for students at different grade levels. In general, the activities in this book align with the following standards for students in grades K–3. For more information, visit the CCSSI website at www.corestandards.org.

Reading: Foundational Skills

Print Concepts
- RF.K.1, RF.1.1. Demonstrate understanding of the organization and basic features of print.

Phonics and Word Recognition
- RF.K.3, RF.1.3, RF.2.3, RF.3.3. Know and apply grade-level phonics and word analysis skills in decoding words.

Fluency
- RF.K.4. Read emergent-reader texts with purpose and understanding.
- RF.1.4, RF.2.4, RF.3.4. Read with sufficient accuracy and fluency to support comprehension.

Writing

Production and Distribution of Writing
- W.3.4. Produce writing in which the development and organization are appropriate to task and purpose.
- W.K.5, W.1.5, W.2.5, W.3.5. Focus on a topic and strengthen writing as needed by revising and editing.

Research to Build and Present Knowledge
- W.K.7, W.1.7, W.2.7. Participate in shared research and writing projects.
- W.3.7. Conduct short research projects that build knowledge about a topic.
- W.K.8, W.1.8, W.2.8, W.3.8. Recall information from experiences or gather information from provided sources to answer a question.

Range of Writing
- W.3.10. Write routinely over extended time frames (time for research, reflection, and revision) and shorter time frames (a single sitting or a day or two) for a range of discipline-specific tasks, purposes, and audiences.

Speaking & Listening

Comprehension and Collaboration
- SL.K.1, SL.1.1, SL.2.1. Participate in collaborative conversations with diverse partners about grade-level topics and texts with peers and adults in small and larger groups.
- SL.K.2, SL.1.2, SL.2.2, SL.3.2. Recount or describe key ideas or details from a text read aloud or information presented orally or through other media.
- SL.K.3, SL.1.3, SL.2.3, SL.3.3. Ask and answer questions about what a speaker says in order to gather additional information or clarify something that is not understood.

Presentation of Knowledge and Ideas
- SL.K.4, SL.1.4, SL.2.4. Describe people, places, things, and events with relevant details, expressing ideas and feelings clearly.
- SL.K.5, SL.1.5, SL.2.5, SL.3.5. Add drawings or other visual displays to stories or recounts of experiences when appropriate to clarify ideas, thoughts, and feelings.

Language

Conventions of Standard English
- L.K.1, L.1.1, L.2.1, L.3.1. Demonstrate command of the conventions of standard English grammar and usage when writing or speaking.
- L.K.2, L.1.2, L.2.2, L.3.2. Demonstrate command of the conventions of standard English capitalization, punctuation, and spelling when writing.

Knowledge of Language
- L.2.3, L.3.3. Use knowledge of language and its conventions when writing, speaking, reading, or listening.

Vocabulary Acquisition and Use
- L.K.4, L.1.4, L.2.4, L.3.4. Determine or clarify the meaning of unknown and multiple-meaning words and phrases based on grade level reading and content, choosing flexibly from an array of strategies.
- L.K.6, L.1.6, L.2.6, L.3.6. Use words and phrases acquired through conversations, reading and being read to, and responding to texts.

CALENDAR TIME

Getting Started

April

Sunday	Monday	Tuesday	Wednesday	Thursday	Friday	Saturday

19

CALENDAR

★ MARK YOUR CALENDAR

Make photocopies of the calendar grid on page 19 and use it to meet your needs. Consider using the write-on spaces to:

- write the corresponding numerals for each day

- mark and count how many days have passed

- track the weather with stamps or stickers

- note student birthdays

- record homework assignments

- communicate with families about positive behaviors

- remind volunteers about schedules, field trips, shortened days, and so on

CELEBRATIONS THIS MONTH

Whether you post a photocopy of pages 20 through 23 near your class calendar or just turn to these pages for inspiration, you're sure to find lots of information on them to discuss with students. To take celebrating and learning a step further, invite the class to add more to the list. For example, students can add anniversaries of significant events and the birthdays of their favorite authors or historical figures.

 ## CALENDAR HEADER

You can make a photocopy of the header on page 24, color it, and use it as a title for your classroom calendar. You might opt to give the coloring job to a student who has a birthday that month. The student is sure to enjoy seeing his or her artwork each and every day of the month.

 ## BEFORE INTRODUCING WHAT'S THE WEATHER?

Make a photocopy of the body template on page 25. Laminate it so you can use it again and again. Before sharing the template with the class, cut out pieces of cloth in the shapes of clothing students typically wear this month. For example, if you live in a warm weather climate, your April attire might include shorts and t-shirts. If you live in chillier climates, your attire might include a scarf, hat, and coat. Fit the cutouts to the body outline. When the clothing props are made, and you're ready to have students dress the template, display the clothing. Invite the "weather helper of the day" to tell what pieces of clothing he or she would choose to dress appropriately for the weather. (For extra fun, use foam to cut out accessories such as an umbrella, sunhat, and raincoat.

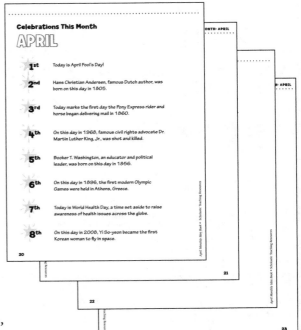

April

Sunday	Monday	Tuesday	Wednesday	Thursday	Friday	Saturday

Celebrations This Month

APRIL

1st   Today is April Fool's Day!

2nd   Hans Christian Andersen, famous Dutch author, was born on this day in 1805.

3rd   Today marks the first day the Pony Express rider and horse began delivering mail in 1860.

4th   On this day in 1968, famous civil rights advocate Dr. Martin Luther King, Jr., was shot and killed.

5th   Booker T. Washington, an educator and political leader, was born on this day in 1856.

6th   On this day in 1896, the first modern Olympic Games were held in Athens, Greece.

7th   Today is World Health Day, a time set aside to raise awareness of health issues across the globe.

8th   On this day in 2008, Yi So-yeon became the first Korean woman to fly in space.

9th This is the day in 1867 that American architect and interior designer Frank Lloyd Wright was born.

10th On this day in 1872, Nebraskans celebrated the first Arbor Day by planting more than 10 million trees throughout the state.

11th The original *Apple* computer was released on this day in 1976.

12th Soviet cosmonaut Yuri Gagarin became the first man in space on this day in 1961.

13th Today is the birth date of Thomas Jefferson, the third president of the United States, who was born in 1743.

14th Noah Webster, Jr., published the first edition of *Webster's American Dictionary* in 1828 and registered the copyright for his book on April 14.

15th On this day in 1947, Jackie Robinson made his debut as the first black Major League baseball player.

16th Harriet Quimby became the first woman to fly an airplane over the English Channel on this day in 1912.

17th The instantly popular Ford *Mustang*, the first "pony car," was introduced at the World's Fair in New York on this day in 1964.

18th On this day in 1775, American patriot Paul Revere set out on his famous ride to warn of the British invasion.

19th Fifteen runners participated in the first Boston Marathon, which was held on this day in 1897.

20th Vitaphone, a new process that added sound to motion pictures was introduced on this day in 1926.

21st On this day in 1838, naturalist and environmental activist John Muir was born.

22nd Today is Earth Day, a day dedicated to raising awareness and appreciation of our natural environment.

23rd Today marks the birth date of English poet and playwright William Shakespeare, born in 1564.

24th The first American newspaper, The *Boston News-Letter*, was published on this day in 1704.

25th On this day in 1990, the Hubble Space Telescope was launched. It remains in operation today, sending images from space back to Earth.

26th John James Audubon, a naturalist, painter, and ornithologist, was born on this day in 1785.

27th Today marks the birth date of Ulysses S. Grant, the 18th president of the United States, who was born in 1822.

28th James Monroe, one of the Founding Fathers of our country and fifth President of the United States, was born on this day in 1758.

29th On this day in 1970, world-renowned tennis player Andre Agassi was born.

30th George Washington was sworn in as the first president of the United States of America on this day in 1789.

APRIL FOOL'S DAY

The first day of April is known by at least two names: All Fool's Day and April Fool's Day. Some believe the day takes its name from celebrations around the time of the spring equinox, when Mother Nature seems to fool us with her unpredictable weather. People in France, however, trace the holiday back to about 1582 when the calendar was reformed under Charles IX. The change meant that the New Year would be observed at the beginning of January rather than April, which had been the custom. Because communication was slow in those times, some were not aware of the change, while others simply refused to accept it. Often, pranksters played tricks on such people, labeling them "April Fish," because they were as naïve as young fish that could easily be caught. In fact, one common prank was to hook paper fish onto the back of people's clothing. Nowadays, whether on April 1st or another day of the month, a few fun, silly activities here and there are a sure way to make learning more exciting for children.

Suggested Activities

 ## PRANKSTER PLANNING PAGE

April Fool's Day is a time when people enjoy playing pranks and practical jokes on others. Explain that these acts are typically lighthearted, harmless tricks that are fun to take part in and funny when the trick is exposed. Ask students if they have ever been "pranked," or had a practical joke played on them. Invite them to share their experiences: how the prank played out, who took part, how it ended, and how they felt when they discovered they had been tricked. Afterward, distribute photocopies of page 30. Have students use the page to describe a prank played on them personally, or one played on someone else, whether in real life, a story, or a movie or television show.

To take the activity a step further, invite students to help plan and carry out a class prank to be played on the whole school! For example, students might decide to wear their clothes backward or inside out on a specific day. When others point out their unusual attire, students could tell them that it's a tradition to wear clothing in that way to express school spirit. Throughout the day, students will find it fun and amusing to see how many schoolmates fall for the prank before being told that it's just a practical joke!

RIDDLE WRITERS

Invite students to write a special kind of problem or puzzle called a riddle. Most riddles are constructed by providing clues or hints in question form that help a person figure out a hidden, and usually humorous, meaning. The riddle solver must use his or her problem-solving abilities, knowledge, and sense of humor to find the solution. To give students practice in deconstructing riddles, ask them to share riddles with which they are familiar. As a class, discuss the parts of each riddle. For example, consider the following riddle:

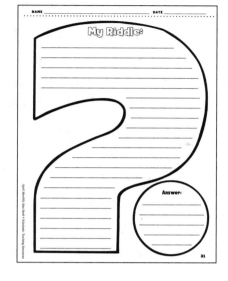

Riddle: What letter can you drink?
Answer: T

After sharing the riddle with students, point out that the clues in the question are the words "letter" and "drink." Explain that the mention of "letter" draws on the riddle solver's knowledge of alphabet letters. The word "drink" signals that he or she should think about letters in a different way. In this case, the riddle solver must be aware of homophones: The phoneme for the letter *T* has the same sound as the word for the beverage *tea*.

After examining several riddles in this way, have students make up their own riddles. Before they begin, help them brainstorm a list of topics that might inspire humorous ideas, such as bananas, bubbles, coconuts, hippopotami, and opossums. Then distribute photocopies of page 31. Have students write their riddle on the question mark and its answer on the period. (More advanced students might enjoy adding the element of rhyme to their riddles, in which one or more clues rhyme with the riddle's solution.) When finished, encourage students to share their riddles with small groups or the whole class.

To create an entertaining, interactive bulletin board, ask students to cut out the question marks and periods on their pages. Collect the cutouts and attach them randomly to a bulletin board. Then challenge students to read each riddle and try to find the corresponding answer.

JACK-IN-THE-BOX RIDDLES

This pop-up clown provides students with a fun way to share their favorite riddles. Photocopy a class supply of pages 32–33. Then distribute a set of pages to each student along with crayons and scissors. To make a jack-in-the-box, have students do the following:

1. Write a riddle on the wind-up box and its answer on the spring.

2. Color and cut out the patterns. Then carefully cut along the vertical dashed lines on the box to make four slits.

3. Insert the tabs on the clown through the slits, as shown.

4. Slide the clown down to cover the answer.

After students complete their jack-in-the-boxes, have them exchange their projects with partners. To use, students read the riddle, try to solve it, then slide the clown up to reveal the answer on the spring.

COMIC-STRIP CREATIONS

Comic strips provide entertaining ways to depict humorous events, stories, or activities (such as practical jokes or pranks). To introduce the topic, bring in some comic strips to share with students. If desired, display the images on an overhead projector or interactive whiteboard. Then point out specific features of the comics, such as the characters' facial expressions, the shape of speech or thought bubbles, and fonts used to depict inflection or emotions in the dialogue. Next, display a photocopy of the charts on pages 34 and 35. Tell students that the symbol chart includes examples of graphics that cartoonists use to show different emotions or ideas. The other chart shows ways they might draw facial features to express a variety of emotions. Explain that cartoonists use many kinds of graphics to help them tell the comic-strip stories they create. Finally, distribute photocopies of page 36 for

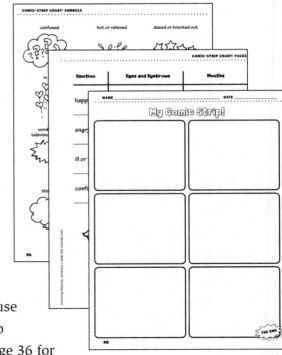

students to use in creating their own comic strips. Before they begin drawing, encourage students to think about what they want their comic strip to be about and the characters they will feature in it. When students are ready to create their comics, they can refer to the symbol and face charts for ideas and inspiration as they draw.

★ FUNNY FACE FILL-INS

Students can make these funny faces to practice drawing facial features that express different emotions. To begin, distribute photocopies of page 37. Then have students draw eyes on the top section, a nose on the middle section, and a mouth on the bottom section. Encourage them to draw features that depict a particular emotion, such as happiness, fear, or surprise. When finished, have students cut out their face patterns and then cut them into three parts along the dashed lines. They can swap sections of their face cutouts with other students to create a variety of funny faces!

★ JUST JOKING!

Tell students that while a riddle provides clues that help one solve a "mystery," a joke is a funny story that has a punch line or humorous twist to it. A joke often includes information such as *who, what, when, where,* and *why*. Share a joke or two with students, or invite them to share a few jokes they know. Then distribute photocopies of the stationery on page 38. Invite students to write a joke they are familiar with on the page, or to make up their own. Afterward, collect students' pages and compile them into a class book, stapling them behind a copy of the book cover on page 39. Write the class name on the author line, then invite a volunteer to color the cover. When the book is completed, place it in the class library for students to enjoy. If desired, you might distribute additional copies of the stationery to students, as well as copies of the cover, and invite them to create their own joke books.

Pranked!

Tell about a practical joke that was played on you or someone else.

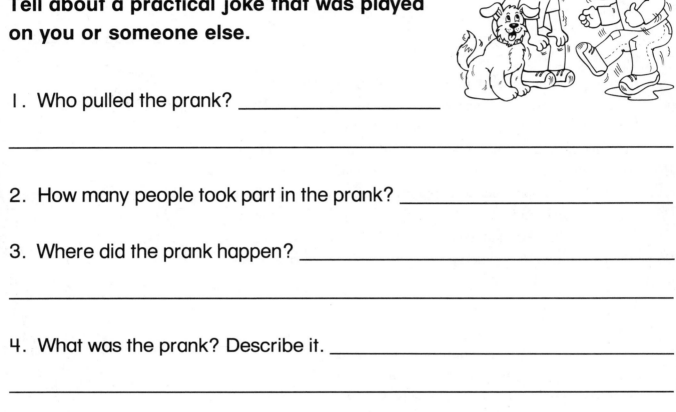

1. Who pulled the prank? _____

_____

2. How many people took part in the prank? _____

3. Where did the prank happen? _____

_____

4. What was the prank? Describe it. _____

_____

_____

5. Did the prank work? ❏ yes ❏ no ❏ not sure

6. What happened when the prank was revealed? _____

_____

_____

_____

On the back of this page, draw a picture of how you, or the pranked person, reacted.

My Riddle:

_____
_____
_____
_____
_____
_____
_____
_____
_____
_____
_____
_____

Answer:

_____
_____
_____

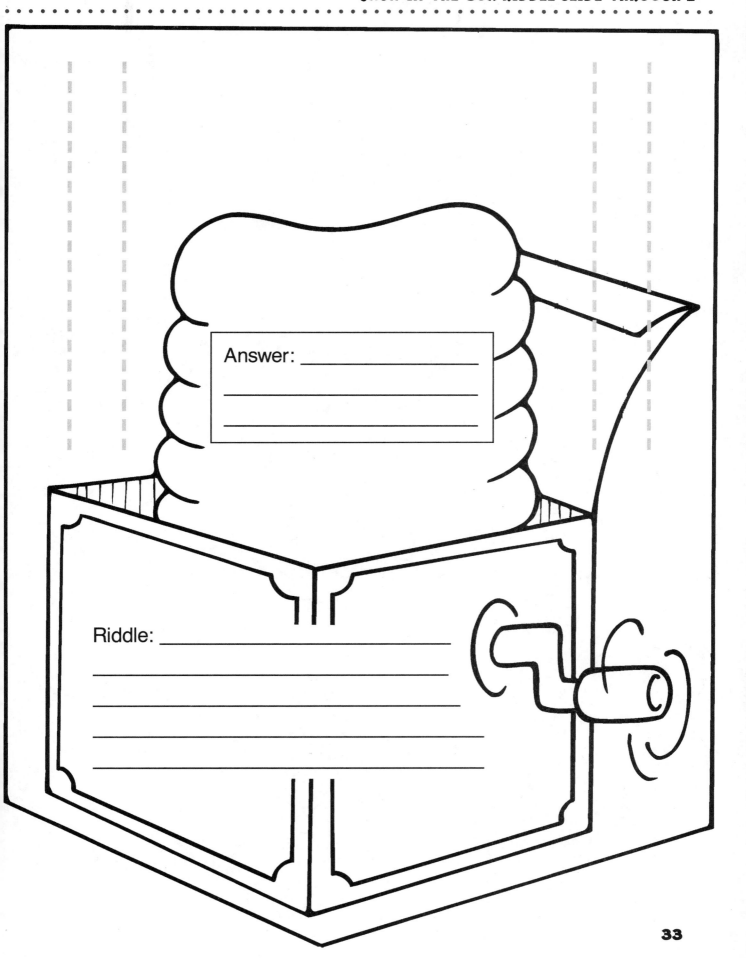

Answer: _____
_____
_____

Riddle: _____
_____
_____
_____
_____

confused

hot or relieved

dazed or knocked out

in love

sleeping

frustrated

words from
television or radio

a great idea

shiny or bright

thinking

sad or gloomy

shivering or cold

Emotion	Eyes and Eyebrows		Mouths	
happy				
angry				
ill or tired				
confused				

My Comic Strip!

THE END

_____'s

Joke Book

ENVIRONMENTAL AWARENESS

Earth Day

This holiday had its beginnings in Wisconsin in 1970, where environmentalist and United States Senator Gaylord Nelson helped coordinate events to raise public awareness about important conservation issues. Now celebrated on April 22 each year, Earth Day is observed around the world by more than a hundred countries. In 2009, the United Nations designated April 22 as International Mother Earth Day.

Arbor Day

In 1872, the country's first Arbor Day was observed due to the efforts of a man named Julius Sterling Morton. A former U.S. Secretary of Agriculture, Morton felt strongly that all citizens needed to take a more active interest in the earth's natural resources, particularly its trees.

In most places in the United States, National Arbor Day is observed on the last Friday in April. On this day, many schools and civic organizations plant trees in an effort to beautify school grounds, neighborhood parks, and other public areas. Many other countries around the world also celebrate Arbor Day, with dates varying and often based on their planting seasons.

Suggested Activities

★ LEAFY LEARNING

One gift that we enjoy from trees is their leaves, which offer shade and beauty to our world. Leaves also provide shelter and sustenance to many kinds of animals. As part of your Earth Day or Arbor Day observances, use the leaf patterns on page 45 for a variety of classroom activities. Simply copy, color, and cut out a supply of the patterns. Then use them for calendar symbols, flash cards, sorting or patterning practice, or manipulatives for math activities. Or, you might use an overhead projector to trace large images of the patterns onto poster board or bulletin board paper to create leaves that can be used in your Earth Day or Arbor Day displays.

★ FOCUS ON FAMILIAR TREES

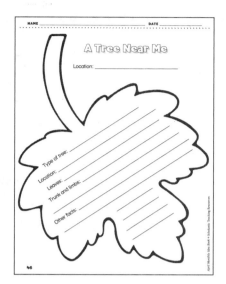

To raise awareness of trees, take your class on a nature walk, encouraging students to share their observations about trees that are on or near the school grounds. You might ask volunteers to point out the shape of a tree's canopy (treetop), its height, the texture of its bark, the color and shape of its leaves, and so on. Before returning to the classroom, choose several trees for students to study more thoroughly. You might take digital photos of each one to use as part of your classroom activities.

Back in the room, divide students into small groups. Assign each group one of the trees from your nature walk. Then distribute photocopies of page 46 to students and have them fill in the location of their tree. Explain that they will use their own observations to complete the page, as well as do research—using the Internet, library books, and other sources—to learn more about their trees. (You might take students back outdoors to visit their trees and make further observations that they can use to fill in their pages.) Encourage the students in each group to work together, sharing their observations and findings with each other. Students can write additional information and facts about their trees on the back of their pages or on another sheet of paper.

Most groups will need a few days to complete their research for this assignment. Once the groups finish their assignments, ask a volunteer from each group to share the group's findings about its tree with the class. Then collect students' pages and bind them behind a photocopy of the book cover on page 47 to make a collaborative class book about the trees. Add a title and author line to the cover, then invite a student to color it. You might create divider pages to place between the pages for each group, using a photo of that group's tree on the divider page. If desired, have students write and draw additional observations about their trees throughout the year, and add their pages to the class book.

CULTIVATING EARTH-CONSCIOUS KIDS

Ask students to collect printed articles and other information about the earth's environment and the efforts of individuals or groups to care for and protect the environment. Be sure to include articles about kids' involvement in environmental projects. You can organize the articles on a bulletin board by dividing it into four sections and labeling each section with a heading, such as "Air," "Land," "Water," and "Animals." Invite students to sort the articles and attach them to the section that best corresponds to their topics. Then discuss the articles with the class and talk about things students might be able to do personally to help care for and protect the environment.

When you are ready to change the display, remove the articles, attach them to plain sheets of paper, and bind the pages to a photocopy of the book cover on page 48. Invite a few volunteers to color the cover. Then place the book in your class library.

 ## FRIEND-OF-THE-EARTH PLEDGES

Invite students to make a pledge promising to help care for the Earth and our environment. To begin, photocopy a class supply of the pledge forms on page 49. Tell students that people often make pledges to do things to help improve their lives, community, or environment. Then distribute the pledges, explaining that students can write a pledge to do what they can to help keep our planet a beautiful and safe place for all of its inhabitants. After they write their pledges, encourage students to draw a few things related to their pledge on the back of their forms. For example, they might draw some ways in which they used recyclable containers in craft projects.

★ EARTH DAY SEND-HOME LETTER

You can invite families to support their child's efforts by sharing details on what students are learning about Earth Day (or Arbor Day) in the classroom. Simply write a letter to parents on a photocopy of page 50, then copy a class supply of the letter to send home with students. For an earth-friendly way to transfer the information, you might scan the letter and email it to parents, or post the file to your class website for parents to download.

★ RECYCLING LOG

Discuss with students the alternatives to placing some items in the trash. Explain that many products today are made from recyclable materials. Invite students to share what they know about recycling in their homes, school, and community. During the discussion, point out that some items can also be reused. Tell students that recycling and reusing items is an environmentally friendly practice that helps reduce the amount of trash that gets sent to the landfills. Then challenge students to brainstorm creative ways they might recycle common household items, such as egg cartons, newspapers, drink cartons, cardboard tubes, and plastic containers. Distribute photocopies of page 51 for students to use to record their recycling activities at home. Ask them to bring in their completed logs to share with the class. Or, set aside a specific day on which students can share and compare their logs, as well as brainstorm additional ways to recycle (or reuse) items.

★ EARTH-DAY READING VINE

Photocopy a supply of the book report form (page 52) onto green paper. Distribute the copies and explain that students will select and read books on Earth-Day or Arbor-Day related topics. After they read a book, have students write a report about it by filling out the form. To create a reading vine, suspend a length of green yarn or nylon rope from the ceiling. Then have students cut out their leaf-shaped reports, attach a length of green yarn or a pipe cleaner to the stem, and hang their leaf from the vine.

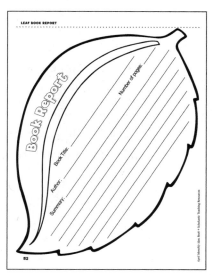

CELEBRATE THE EARTH

Set aside a special time in class to gather students and their families for a celebration to honor the Earth and her many gifts to us. For invitations, fill in the pertinent information on a photocopy of page 53, then make a class supply of the invitations for students to color and take home. In advance, involve students in planning the event. For example, they might help choose and prepare foods and activities that relate to earth, trees, and the environment. Here are some suggestions to consider:

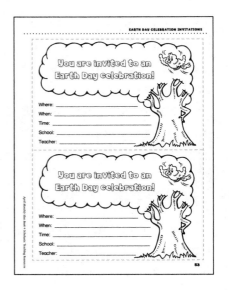

- Locate a tree at the school or nearby park to adopt. Or plant a sapling that students and parents can help take care of all year. Then, during the commemoration, present the tree (or sapling) and lead participants in a pledge expressing their commitment to taking care of it.

- Read poetry and literary excerpts about nature and the environment.

- Renew students' pledges to be a friend of the Earth. Invite families to join in.

- Sing songs or play music related to caring for the Earth.

- Prepare snack foods that come only from trees.

- Use eco-friendly dishes and flatware to serve food and drinks during the event.

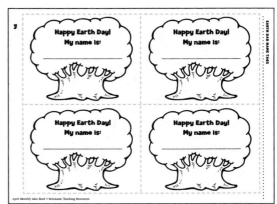

On the day of the celebration, provide photocopies of the name tags on page 54. Make enough name tags for students and their guests. If desired, invite students to color the name tags. Then place them in a basket, and set the basket near the door along with markers and tape. Ask both students and guests to fill out a name tag to wear during the class celebration. They can affix it to their clothing with rolled tape.

NAME ______________________________ DATE ______________

A Tree Near Me

Location: ______________________________

Type of tree: ______________________________

Location: ______________________________

Leaves: ______________________________

Trunk and limbs: ______________________________

____

Other facts: ______________________________

____

PLACE THIS SIDE ALONG FOLD.

We Are
Earth-Conscious Kids

by _____

I am a friend of our planet. To keep Earth and her inhabitants safe and sound, I promise to

_____

_____

_____

_____

_____

_____

I am a friend of our planet. To keep Earth and her inhabitants safe and sound, I promise to

_____

_____

_____

_____

_____

_____

Dear Parents,

_____

_____

_____

_____

_____

_____

_____

_____

_____

_____

Thank you,

_____

Teacher

My Recycling Log

Item	Action

Book Report

Number of pages: _____

Book Title: _____

Author: _____

Summary: _____

You are invited to an Earth Day celebration!

Where: _____

When: _____

Time: _____

School: _____

Teacher: _____

You are invited to an Earth Day celebration!

Where: _____

When: _____

Time: _____

School: _____

Teacher: _____

CHICKENS & EGGS

Female chickens, or hens, lay eggs to reproduce. An embryo develops inside a chicken egg that has been fertilized. After about three weeks of incubation, a baby chick hatches from the egg, thus beginning a new life. Some hens lay unfertilized eggs—these are the type of eggs that we purchase in grocery stores and use for food.

Symbolism

In many countries around the world, the egg is often a cultural or religious symbol for new life. In some religious observances, such as Easter, eggs are decorated with colorful designs and patterns. In Europe, pysanky eggs (or Ukrainian Easter eggs) are painted in intricate folk designs using traditional colors and patterns. Many other European cultural groups also decorate eggs for Easter, using a variety of methods. In the United States, communities and families often follow the tradition of dyeing hard-boiled eggs with food coloring and then hiding them outdoors for young children to find. The most famous Easter egg hunt, usually held the Saturday before Easter Sunday, takes place on the lawn of the White House in Washington, DC.

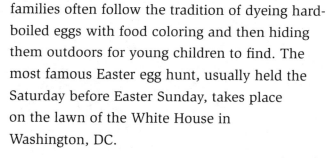

Suggested Activities

★ "INSIDE AN EGG" MINI-BOOK

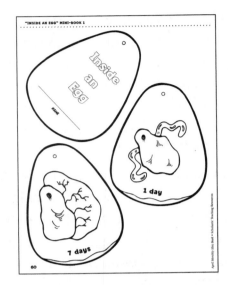

Introduce students to the stages of a chick's development with this egg-shaped mini-book. To prepare, photocopy a class set of the mini-book pages (pages 60–61) and distribute one set to each student. Provide scissors and brass fasteners, then have students do the following to assemble their books:

1. Cut out each page.

2. Punch a hole at the top of each page where indicated.

3. Sequence the pages in numerical order, starting with the page labeled "1 day" and ending with the page with "21 days." Stack the pages and top them with the cover.

4. Check that the holes at the top of the pages are aligned. Then use a brass fastener to bind the pages together.

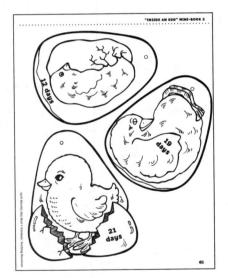

After students have assembled their mini-books, review the pages with them one at a time. Talk about how the chick in the egg changes over time. If desired, provide a book or poster that features colored pictures of the development of a baby chick. Then invite students to use the pictures as a guide to color the developing chick on their mini-book pages. To complete, have them write their name on the cover. Finally, invite students to take their mini-books home to share with their families and friends.

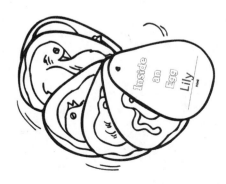

CHICKEN FACT HATCHERS

Have students conduct research to gather facts about chickens. Encourage them to use the Internet, school and local library books, and other sources to do their research. As students discover different facts about these domestic birds, ask them to jot down their findings on a sheet of paper. After completing their research, give students one photocopy of page 62, two copies of page 63, and five brass fasteners. Then have them do the following to assemble a chicken fact hatcher:

1. Cut out each pattern. Then cut apart only one of the egg patterns along the zigzag line. These will be the chicken's wings. The other egg will be used for the chicken's body.

2. Color the chicken, legs, and wings (the two egg halves).

3. Turn over the body (the whole, uncut egg). On the back, write one or two facts about chickens, using information from the research that was done.

4. Using brass fasteners, attach the chicken head, legs, and wings to the body, as shown. Check that the text on the body is face up when attaching the parts of the chicken to it. (Students can use the markings on the back of the body as a guide for placing and attaching the pieces.)

5. Fold the head and legs forward onto the large egg, then fold the wings over them so that they cover the entire body.

After students assemble their projects, invite them to exchange "eggs" with partners. To use, have students unfold the parts in reverse order (wings, legs, then head) to reveal the chicken facts on the body.

ON-THE-NEST WORD FIND

Distribute copies of the word find on page 64 to reinforce what students have learned about chickens and eggs. After students complete the activity, invite them to color the picture on the front, then turn their page over to write a creative story about what it might be like to be a chick, hen, or rooster. Encourage students to use words from their puzzle as they write.

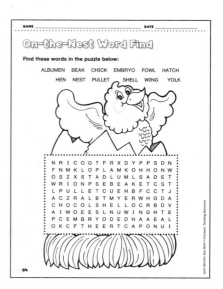

★ INVESTIGATING CHICKENS

To extend students' knowledge of chickens, invite them to conduct additional research, including egg production and the development of chicks. Or, consider having them research the role of chickens and eggs in the health and nutrition of humans. Encourage students to use the Internet, library books, and other sources to do their research. Then have students use their findings to write a report about their chosen topic. (Most students will need a few days to complete this assignment.) You can distribute photocopies of the stationery on page 65 for students to use for their final drafts. If desired, also give students copies of page 66 for them to use as a cover for their reports. Have them add a title and author line to their cover and then color it.

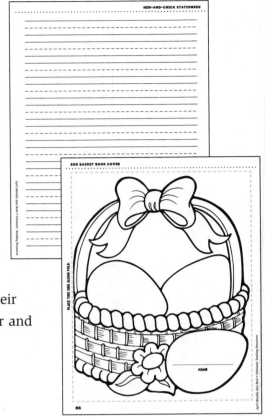

★ CHICKEN BULLETIN-BOARD TOPPER

For another way to present students' research on chickens (see "Investigating Chickens"), prepare a bulletin board topped with a friendly chicken. To make the chicken, enlarge the head and wing patterns on pages 67 and 68 onto poster board. Then attach the pieces to the top of a bulletin board, as shown. If desired, students can write the final drafts of their reports on copies of the stationery on page 69. When finished, help them display their pages on the bulletin board below the chicken. Add a title, such as "Good Eggs!" to complete the display.

HATCH-A-SKILL EGGS

These hinged eggs make great center activities that can be used to reinforce a variety of skills. To assemble, cut out construction-paper copies of the egg and chick patterns on page 70. (Make as many copies as you need for the skill you plan to teach.) Program the two egg halves with the skill you want to teach and write the answer on the chick. Use a brass fastener to attach the pieces together, as shown. To use, students read the task, give their response, then separate the two halves of the egg to check their answer.

If desired, invite students to make their own hinged eggs. They might label the two shells with a seasonal greeting (related to spring, Easter, or another spring event) and write a special message on the chick. Or, they might write a chicken-related riddle and its answer on the pieces.

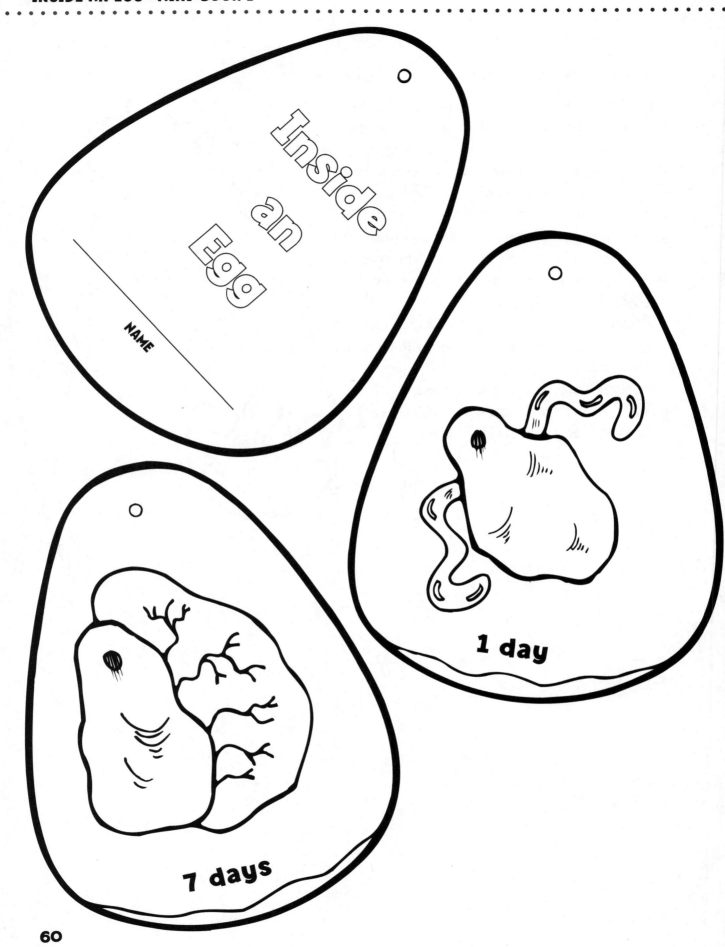

Inside
an
Egg

NAME

1 day

7 days

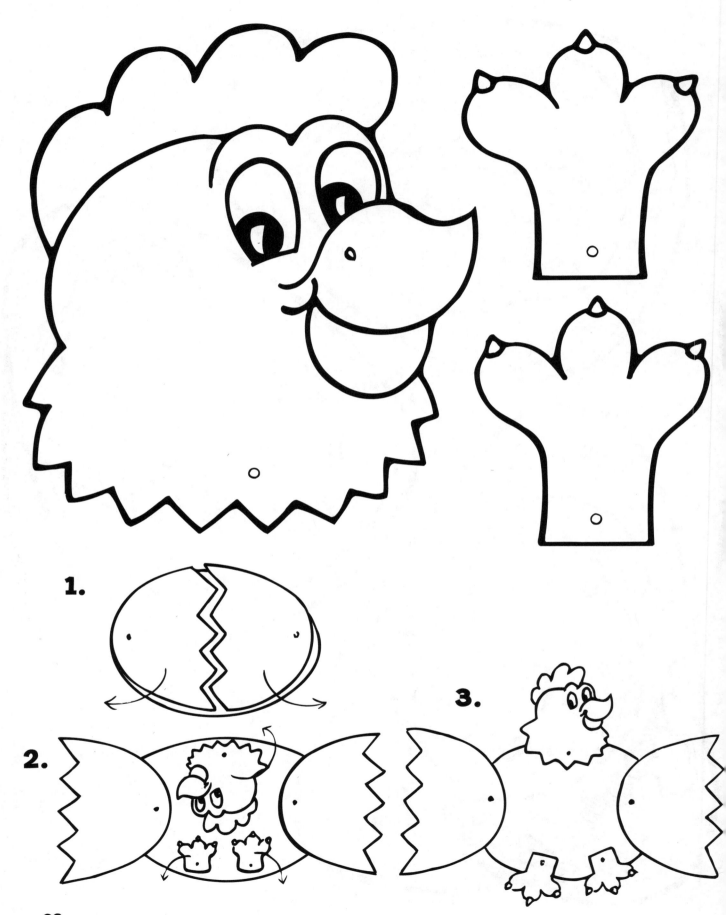

1.

2.

3.

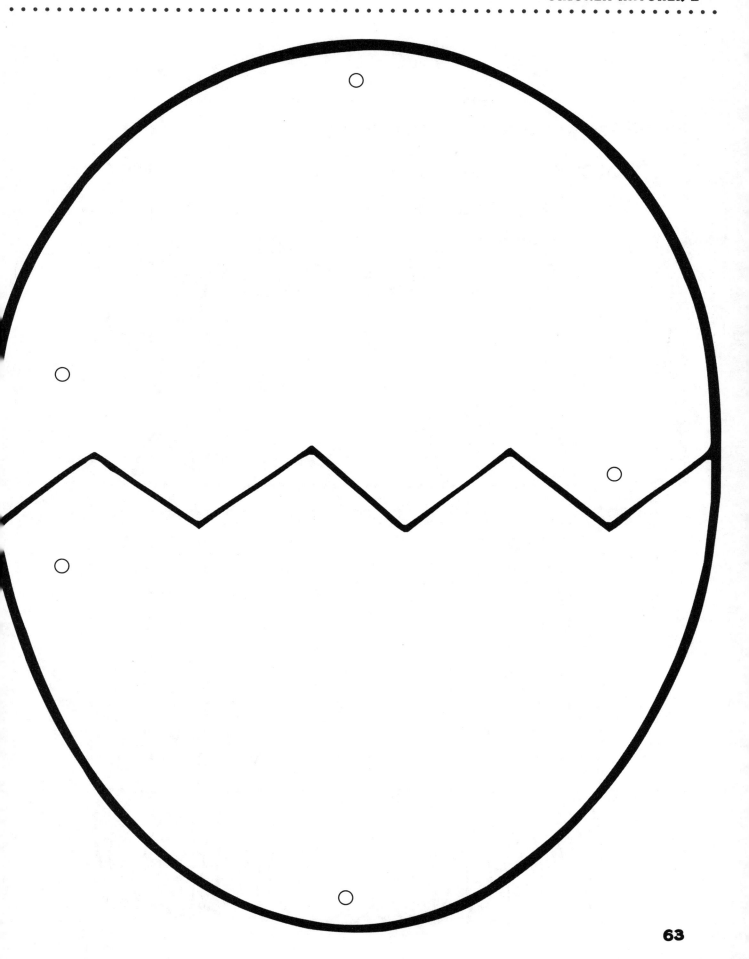

On-the-Nest Word Find

Find these words in the puzzle below:

ALBUMEN   BEAK   CHICK   EMBRYO   FOWL   HATCH

HEN   NEST   PULLET   SHELL   WING   YOLK

```
N R I C O G T F R X D Y P P S D N
F N M K L O P L A M K O H H O N W
O S Z X S T A D L U M L S A D E T
W R I O N P S E B E A K E T C S T
L P U L L E T C U E H B F C C T J
A C Z R A L B T M Y E R W H G D A
C H O C O L S H E L L O C R B D V
A I W O E E S L N U W I N G H T E
P C E M B R Y O D E D H A A E A L
O K C F T H E E R T C A P O N U I
```

PLACE THIS SIDE ALONG FOLD.

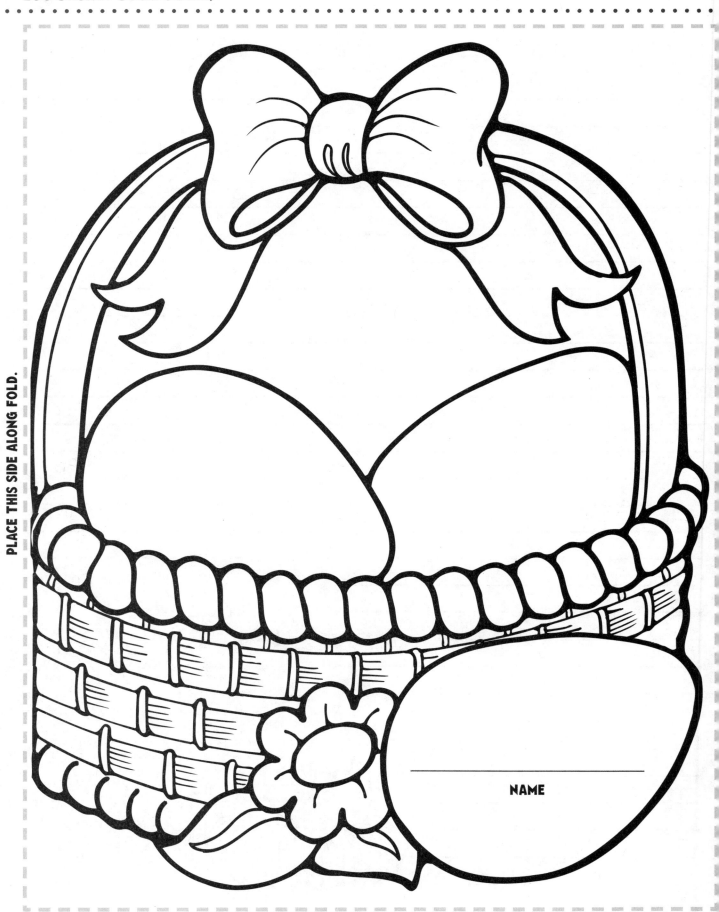

NAME

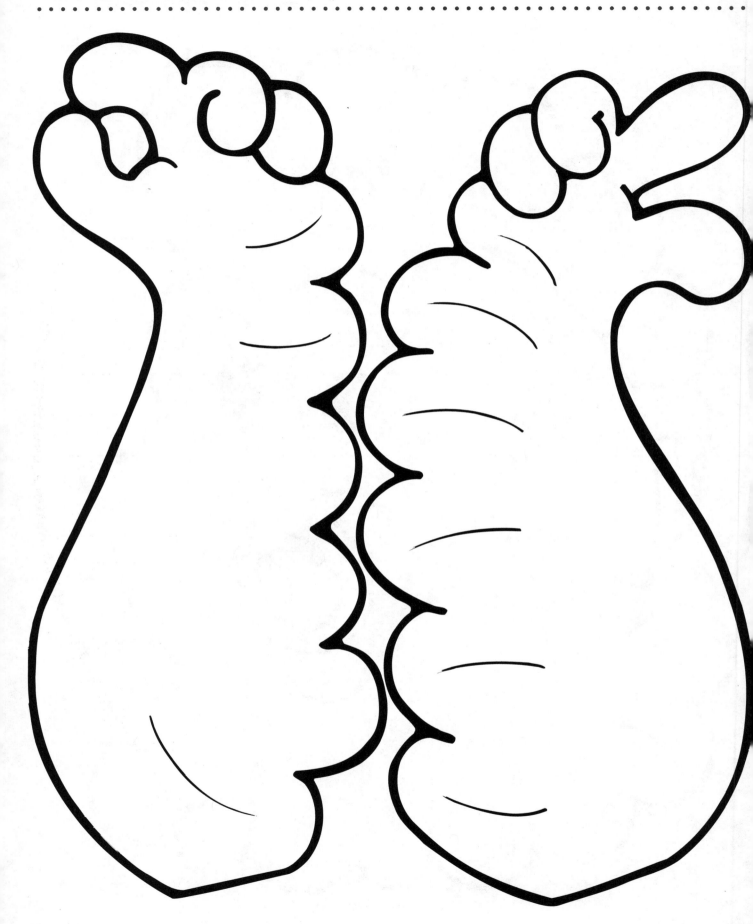

BUNNY RABBITS

Rabbits are plant-eating animals that live in the wild in many parts of the world, including forests, grasslands, deserts, and wetlands. These mammals are highly adaptable to new environments. A male rabbit is called a buck and a female is a doe. Rabbits give birth to several litters during a breeding season, producing from four to twelve babies, or kittens, in each litter. Since the breeding season for most rabbits lasts nine months, one female rabbit could have several dozen kittens within a year's time.

Due to their rapid reproduction rates, rabbits are often used as a symbol of fertility and new life in association with spring and Easter. In the United States, rabbits are also associated with delivering Easter eggs. This legend arose from a German story about a poor mother, who, during a famine, dyed some Easter eggs for her children and hid them in a nest. Just as the children discovered the eggs, a large rabbit was seen hopping away, as if it had been the one to deliver the eggs to the nest! Over time, the story grew, making the Easter bunny a tradition in many Easter observances.

Suggested Activities

★ RABBIT PAPER-BAG PUPPET

Invite students to make puppets to use for their rabbit role-playing and dramatizations. To begin, distribute a small paper bag and a photocopy of the rabbit patterns on page 75 to each student. Also, provide craft materials such as cotton balls, felt, buttons, and sequins. Then have students do the following to make their puppets:

1. Color and cut out the patterns.

2. Glue the rabbit's head to the bottom flap of the bag. Then glue the bow to the rabbit's chin.

3. Use craft items to add embellishments to the puppet. For example, cotton balls could be glued on the rabbit's head, sequins could be glued to the bow, and buttons added to the "body" (front of paper bag).

★ MR. BUNNY PAGE FRAMER

Rabbits are fascinating animals that are sure to inspire students' imagination and creativity. Encourage students to write short stories, skits, poems, songs, or other text about rabbits. Or, have them draw imaginative pictures or cartoons of these creatures. When students complete their work, distribute photocopies of the rabbit patterns on page 76. To make a page framer, ask students to color and cut out the patterns, then glue the rabbit's head, hands, and feet to the edges of a sheet of construction paper. Finally, have them attach their written work or drawing to the front of the page framer.

★ 10-CARROT FACT BOOK

Ask students to use sources such as the Internet and nonfiction library books to research rabbits. As they discover different facts about rabbits, have students write their findings on a sheet of paper. Encourage them to search for ten or more facts. Then distribute photocopies of the carrot pattern on page 77. To make fact books about rabbits, have students do the following:

1. Cut out the pattern. Use it as a template to cut out ten carrot-shaped pages from plain paper.

2. Write a different rabbit fact on each page. Add illustrations, if desired.

3. To make the cover, glue the pattern cutout to a sheet of folded construction paper. (Align the top "leafy" edge along the fold.) Then trim the construction paper to the shape of the carrot through both layers.

4. Stack and staple the book pages together between the fold of the cover. Add a title and author line, then color the cover.

If desired, create an interactive bulletin board to showcase students' books. To prepare, cover the bottom half of a bulletin board with brown paper to represent garden soil and the top with blue paper for the sky. Then cut slits in the soil, each one about the same width as the middle of one of the carrot books. "Plant" each student's book in the garden by inserting it into a slit. To use, invite students or guests to remove books from the display to read, then return them when finished.

★ RABBIT POP-UP PUPPET

Students can make pop-up puppets to use as props when presenting information about rabbits—or just for fun! Provide small groups with photocopies of the rabbit patterns (page 78), craft sticks, paper cups, glue, and green construction paper. To make a pop-up puppet, have each student do the following:

1. Color and cut out a rabbit pattern. Glue the cutout to a craft-stick handle.

2. Make a one-inch slit in the bottom of a cup.

3. Cut a 2-inch wide strip of green construction paper, making it long enough to fit around the cup rim.

4. Fringe one long edge of the paper strip. Glue the strip—fringe end up—around the top edge of the cup, as shown.

5. From the inside of the cup, poke the puppet handle through the slit in the cup bottom.

6. Slide the handle up and down to make the rabbit hop!

★ HOPPING BUNNIES

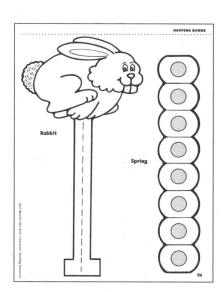

Reinforce graphing with this movement activity. First, divide the class into small groups, each with the same number of students. Explain that each student will take a turn hopping like a bunny. Then have group members keep count as a student hops in place as many times as possible in a designated amount of time, such as one minute (use a stopwatch or timer). After every student has had a turn to hop, have students add the total number of hops for their group. Use the results to create a class graph. Then have students use the graph to answer questions, such as "Which group had the most hops?" and "How many times did groups A and B hop all together?"

As a follow-up, invite students to make a hopping bunny. Distribute photocopies of the patterns on page 79, provide scissors and hole punches, then have students do the following to make the project:

1. Cut out the rabbit and spring patterns.

2. Use a hole punch to remove the shaded circles from the spring. (Younger students may need help punching enough holes to remove each circle entirely.)

3. Fanfold the spring, folding on each of the solid lines.

4. Fold and crease the dashed line on the rabbit "handle." Insert the handle through the holes in the folded spring.

5. To make the bunny "hop," hold the bottom section of the spring between two fingers. Pull the rabbit handle down through the holes until the rabbit rests against the folds. Then release the handle— the spring will expand and "shoot" the bunny into the air so that it appears to hop!

★ RABBIT SKILLS WHEEL

Use the rabbit wheel patterns on pages 80–81 to reinforce math skills and more. To prepare, write a problem in each of the large boxes (outlined in gray). Write the answer in the small box directly opposite each problem on the right. Cut out the rabbit, carrot, and wheel. Then carefully cut out the "windows" on the rabbit. Use one brass fastener to attach the wheel to the rabbit and another to attach the carrot, as shown. To use, students turn the wheel so that a problem appears in the left window. They solve the problem and then slide the carrot away from the right window to check their answer.

★ "HOPPY" READER'S READING LOG

Give each student a few photocopies of the reading log on page 82. Then explain that students will select and read books about rabbits. In advance, you might want to gather a collection of these books—in a variety of genres—to place in your class library, or work with the media specialist at your school to set up a section in the media center for this purpose. Encourage students to fill out a section on their reading logs for each book they read. After students complete their logs, invite them to tell about their favorite rabbit book and make recommendations to classmates about books they might want to read in the future.

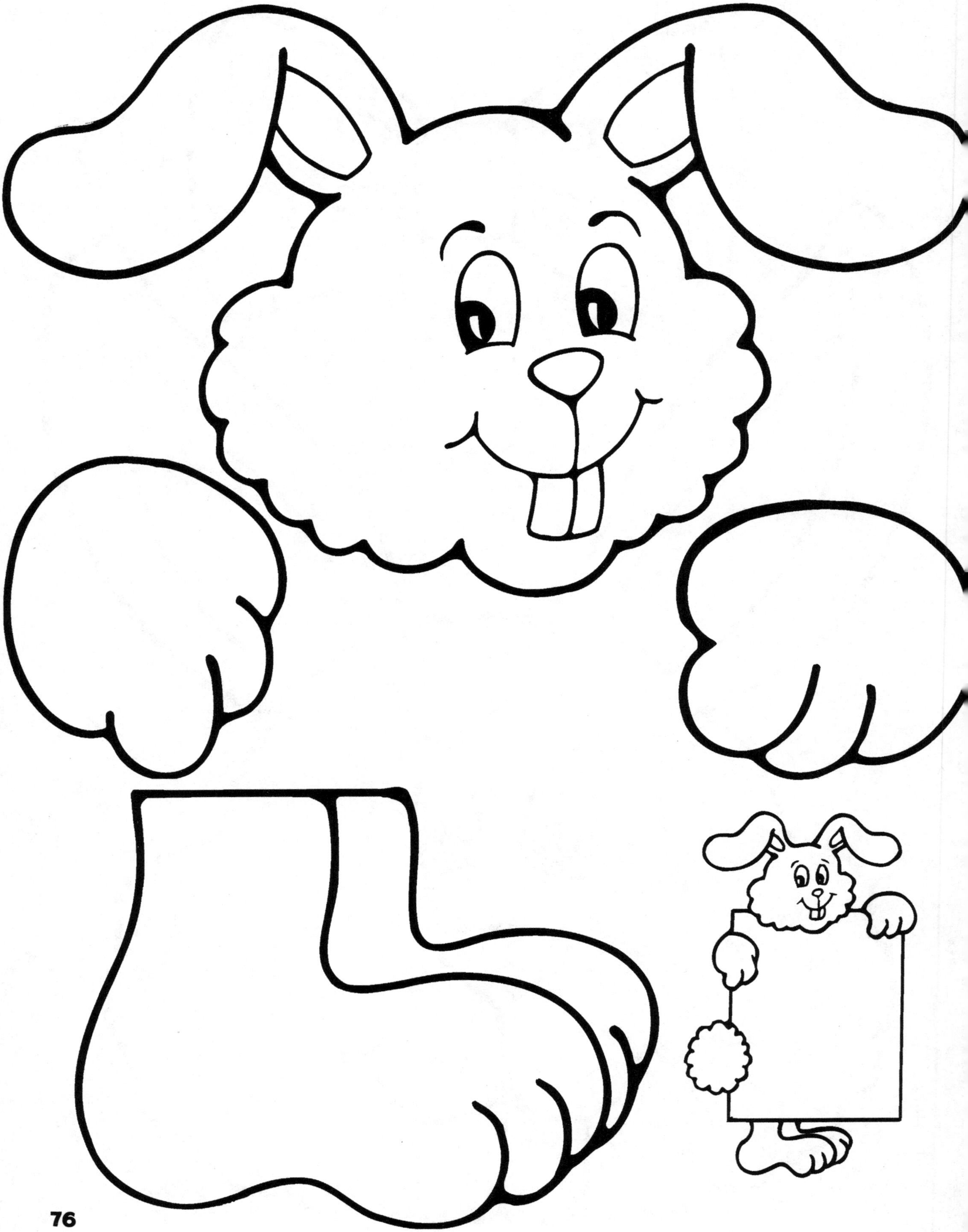

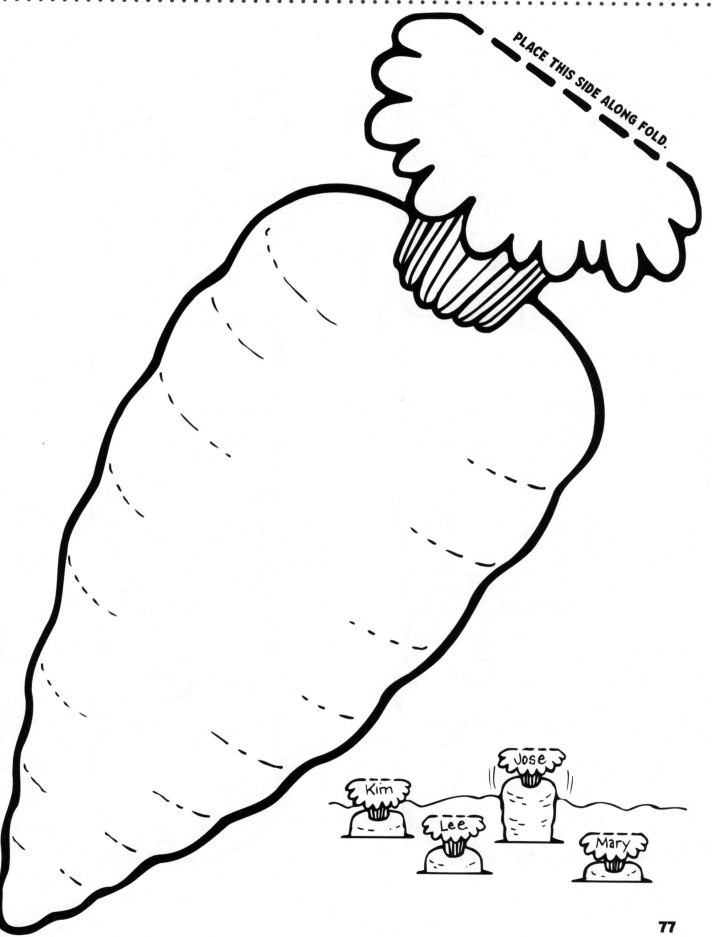

PLACE THIS SIDE ALONG FOLD.

Kim

Jose

Lee

Mary

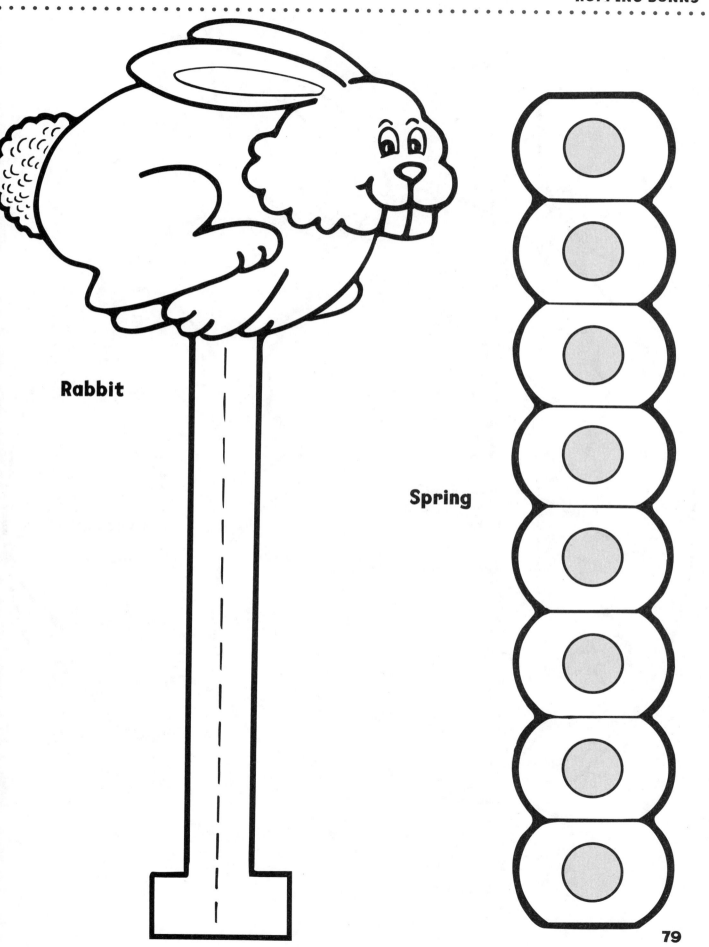

Rabbit

Spring

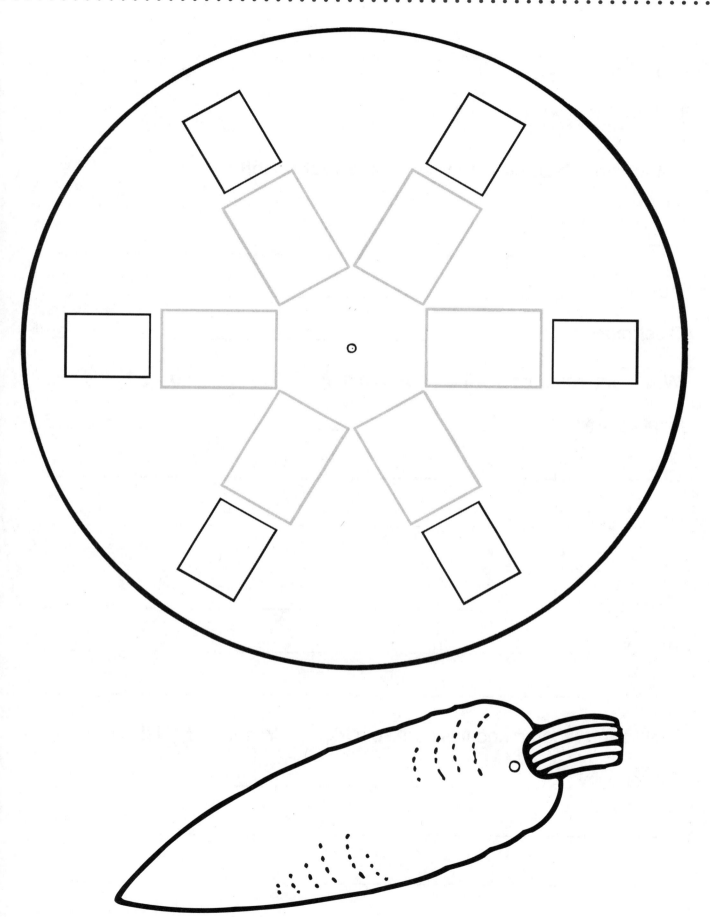

"Hoppy" Reader's Reading Log

Record each book that you read about rabbits or hares.

Title _____

Author _____

Illustrator _____

Would you recommend this book to a friend? Yes ☐   No ☐

Explain why: _____

_____

_____

- -

Title _____

Author _____

Illustrator _____

Would you recommend this book to a friend? Yes ☐   No ☐

Explain why: _____

_____

_____

APRIL SHOWERS

April showers bring May flowers…along with lots of learning opportunities! Rain is one of the basic needs of flowers, contributing to their nutritional requirements and growth. With the activities in this unit, you can help students develop an understanding of the role of rain in plant growth. In addition, they can explore the bounteous blooms that benefit from the rainy days of April.

Suggested Activities

★ RAINY DAYS UMBRELLA

Use this 3-D umbrella to help students keep track of the rainy days that occur during the month of April. To make an umbrella, students color and cut out a photocopy of the canopy and handle patterns on page 88. Then they fold the canopy along each dashed line to create creases. To form the dome shape of the canopy, students tape together the straight edges that extend from the center. Finally, they poke a length of yarn through the top center of the canopy and tape the end on the inside of the canopy to the straight end of the handle. They can tie a loop in the end of the yarn that extends from the top of the umbrella to form a hanger.

To keep track of rainy days, simply invite students to cut out a construction-paper raindrop for each day it rains and label the cutout with the date. Then have them use yarn to hang the raindrop from the umbrella.

★ HOW DOES YOUR GARDEN GROW?

Discuss with students the needs of flowering plants (soil, water, light, and air). Then introduce them to the stages of a flower's development. You might use illustrations from nonfiction books to point out the sequence a flowering plant follows as it grows. Next, photocopy a class supply of the sequencing cards on page 89 and distribute the pages to students. Ask them to color and cut apart the cards. Then have students sequence the cards to show the developmental stages of a flower. They can then add numbers to the bottom right corner of each card, write a brief description about the stage on the back of each card, and bind the cards together to create a mini-book. Or, students might glue the cards, in sequence, onto a large sheet of construction paper and write a description below each one.

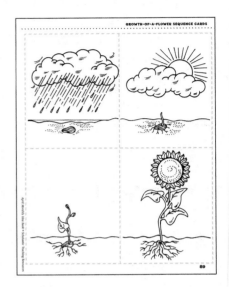

★ APRIL SHOWERS MOBILE

Invite students to create mobiles that represent the connection between rain and flowers. First, photocopy a class supply of the patterns on pages 90–91. Then distribute a set of pages to each student, along with two 1-foot lengths of yarn and scissors. Also provide glue, clear tape, and an assortment of decorative craft items, such as glitter, iridescent tinsel icicles (as used on Christmas trees), and tissue-paper scraps. Then have students do the following to make their mobile:

1. Cut out the umbrella, handle, raindrops, and flower patterns.

2. On the back of the umbrella cutout, write about how rain helps a flower grow. Then tape the handle to the umbrella.

3. Color or decorate the front of each piece. If desired, use craft items to add texture and interest. For example, attach tissue-paper scraps to the umbrella, glue glitter to the flower, and tape a few icicles to the umbrella to represent falling rain.

4. Punch holes in each piece where indicated.

5. Cut one of the 1-foot lengths of yarn into three pieces of varying lengths. Tie one end of a length of yarn to the flower and the other end to the bottom of the umbrella handle. Use the other two lengths of yarn to similarly attach each raindrop to the umbrella, as shown.

6. To make a hanger, tie the other 1-foot length of yarn to the top of the umbrella.

★ WONDERFUL RAIN

Tell students that the rain that falls today is the same water that was on earth thousands and even millions of years ago. Explain that through a process called the water cycle, water is constantly changing forms from precipitation, evaporation, and condensation. Describe the water cycle to students, then invite them to give examples of water in each of the three stages. For instance, rain is an example of precipitation, steam is evaporation, and dew is condensation. After discussing, have students further research the water cycle to learn more about it. Encourage them to use different sources, such as nonfiction books, the Internet, and videos, to do their research. If desired, they might also research other rain-related topics, such as types of clouds or ways to conserve water. After students complete their research, invite them to write a few paragraphs about their findings on photocopies of the stationery on page 92. Finally, invite students to share their written work with the class. Later, you might display students' work on a bulletin board titled "Wonderful Rain!"

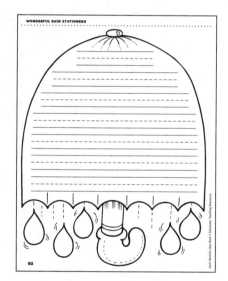

As an extension, students might complete rain-related creative writing assignments on pages of the stationery. For instance, they might use a story-starter such as "I'm a big, plump raindrop hanging from a cloud in the sky" as a springboard to write an imaginary story about a raindrop's journey through the water cycle.

★ FANTASTIC FLOWERS

Discuss with students the parts of a flower (such as the petals, pistil, sepals, stamen, stigma, and stem), and their corresponding functions and locations. Display pictures of different kinds of flowers, including a lily and daffodil, and point out each part during your discussion. Then distribute copies of the flower patterns on pages 93 and 94. Also, provide construction paper, scissors, tape, and glue. Explain that students will use the patterns and other materials to make their own lily and daffodil. Have them follow these directions to make each bloom:

Lily

1. Cut out the lily pattern (page 93).

2. To curl the petals, roll each petal tightly around a pencil, then release by removing the pencil.

3. To complete the bloom, shape the lily into a cone or tube, with the petals curling away from the center. Tape the ends together to secure. (See above.)

Daffodil

1. Cut out the petals and trumpet, or *corona* (page 94).

2. Cut the solid lines along both long edges of the trumpet. Then form a tube by bringing the two short ends together and taping them in place.

3. Fold out the wide tabs at one end of the trumpet, as shown.

4. Center the trumpet onto the petals cutout. Then tape the tabs to the petals. Spread out the fringed end of the corona to complete the daffodil bloom, as shown above.

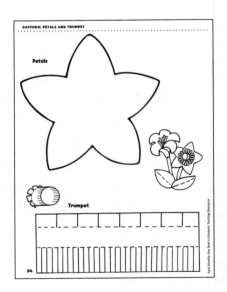

After making each flower bloom, add construction paper features, such as a stigma, stamens, sepals, leaves, and stem.

★ FLOWERY WRITING

Inspire some science-based writing about flowers with this large-bloom stationery. First, have students choose a flower to research. If desired, brainstorm a list of common flowers with students and have them choose their flower from the list. Then have them do research using nonfiction books, the Internet, and other sources to learn about the anatomy, growth, nutritional and environmental needs, and other information about their flower. After students complete their research, have them compile their findings into a report. Distribute photocopies of the stationery (page 95) for students to use for their final drafts. Then invite volunteers to share their reports with the class. Finally, gather and bind the reports together to create a collaborative class book about flowers.

★ BLOOMING FUN GLASSES

Invite students to make and wear a pair of glasses to celebrate the blooming flowers of spring. Distribute copies of the glasses patterns on page 96. Have students color and cut out the patterns, carefully cutting the slits on the glasses frame and the earpieces. To assemble, students simply fit each earpiece into the corresponding slit on the frame. If desired, students can take their glasses home to share with family members.

★ BLOOMING GOOD BOOKS!

Give each student a few photocopies of the reading log on page 97. Explain that students will select and read books about flowers. If desired, gather a collection of flower-related fiction and nonfiction books to put in your class library. Or, help students find flower-related books of interest in the school library. After students read a book, have them fill out a section on their reading logs. Periodically, invite students to share their reading logs with the class and make reading recommendations.

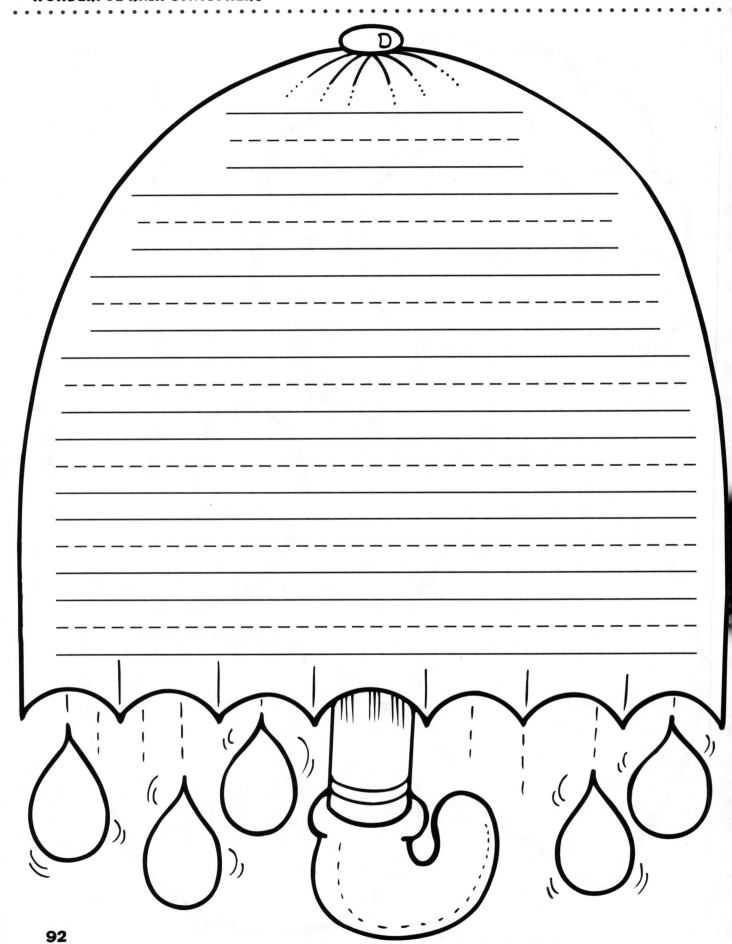

Petals

Trumpet

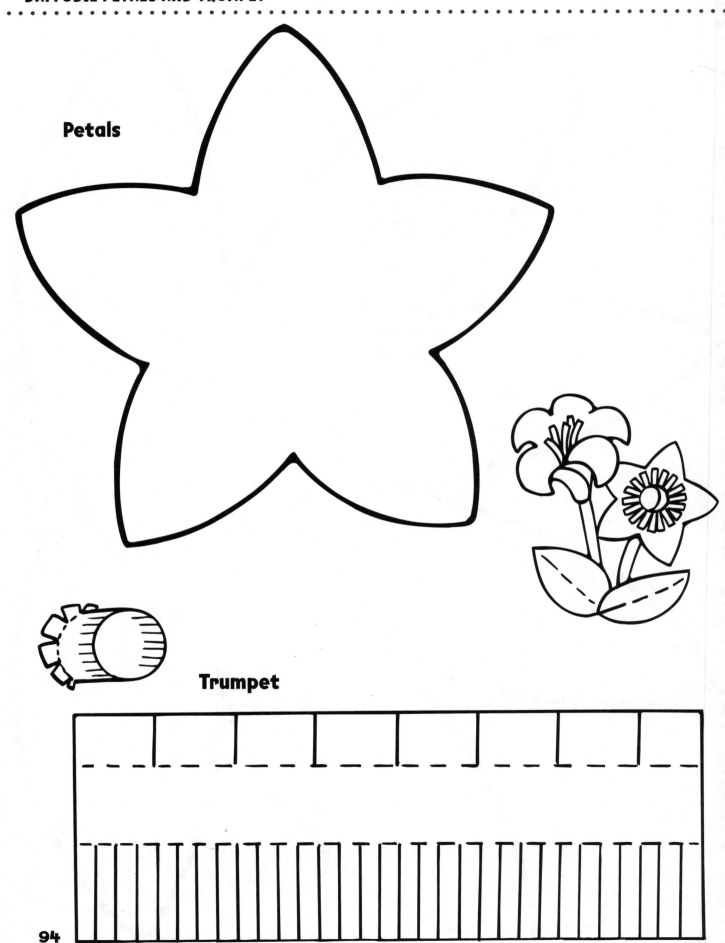

NAME ______________________________ DATE ______________

Blooming Good Books!
Reading Log

Record each book about flowers that you read.

Title ______________________________

Author ______________________________

Illustrator ______________________________

Would you recommend this book to a friend? Yes ❑ No ❑

Explain your reasons: ______________________________

____

____

Title ______________________________

Author ______________________________

Illustrator ______________________________

Would you recommend this book to a friend? Yes ❑ No ❑

Explain your reasons: ______________________________

____

____

INCREDIBLE INSECTS

There are more than a million types of insects around the world, with more being discovered all the time. Butterflies, bees, and ladybugs are only a few of the more commonly known insects found in outdoor public areas and amid flower blooms in gardens. Other places that make popular insect-harbors are trees, fallen logs, rocky areas, leaf piles—and even dark closets inside homes!

Although insects come in many different sizes and shapes, all insects have these body parts in common: a head, thorax, abdomen, antennae, and six legs. Most insects also have eyes and wings. One of the tiniest insects known to man is the fairy fly, a type of wasp that could fit easily through the eye of a needle. One of the largest insects is the grasshopper-like giant weta, which can grow to four inches long and weigh as much as a sparrow.

Suggested Activities

 ★ **STUDYING INSECTS**

Tell students that the study of insects is called entomology. Then introduce students to the characteristics of insects, using "Let's Talk About Insects," an online tutorial sponsored by the University of Illinois Extension at http://urbanext.illinois. edu/insects. (Or, share the information about insects below.) Afterward, distribute photocopies of the diagram (page 105) and have students label the body parts of the grasshopper.

Head: The head usually contains the eyes, mouthparts, and antennae.

Eyes: Most insects have compound eyes, which consist of many lenses. Some have simple eyes that contain a single lens. Insects might have two or more eyes, and some even have both compound and simple eyes!

Mouthparts: The mouthparts vary according to what insects feed on, allowing them to chew, bite, pinch, pierce, or suck their food.

Antennae: These are used to sense sounds, vibrations, smells, and other environmental factors.

Thorax: This is the middle section of an insect's body. The wings and legs are attached to the thorax.

Legs: All insects have three pairs of legs (six legs).

Wings: Most insects have two pairs of wings (four wings), but some have just one pair (two wings) or no wings at all—such as ants and fleas.

Abdomen: This is usually the largest part of an insect's body. It contains vital organs used for digestion, respiration, and reproduction.

★ STAND-UP GRASSHOPPER

Continue your exploration of insects with this stand-up grasshopper. First, ask students to color and cut out tagboard photocopies of the grasshopper patterns on page 106. Have them glue a leg to each side of the abdomen, then fold the body along the dashed line. Students can use sticky flags to label the parts of the grasshopper. To display, stand the grasshopper on a flat surface, such as a tabletop or windowsill. Or, attach them to a display backed with green-fringed bulletin-board paper to represent grass.

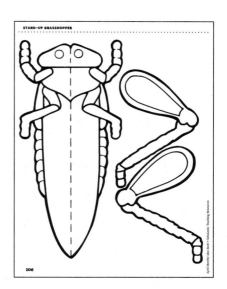

★ INTERESTING INSECTS!

Expand students' knowledge about insects by having them research and write about insects that have unique attributes or skills. For example, students might choose to learn about an insect that migrates or has the ability to pollinate. Encourage students to use a variety of resources to do their research—such as the Internet, nonfiction books, videos, documentaries, and interviews with specialists at the county extension agency. Some students might find useful information for their research by visiting the National Geographic Wild website at http://animals.nationalgeographic.com/animals/bugs. Distribute photocopies of page 107 for students to fill out as they discover facts and other interesting information about their insect. If they need more space to write, they can use the back of the page. (Most children will need a few days to complete the assignment.)

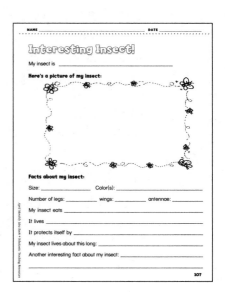

After students complete their pages, invite them to share their findings with the class. If desired, collect the pages and bind them together to create a class book about insects.

★ BEE PUPPET

Pique students' interest in bees with this easy-to-make puppet. To begin, distribute photocopies of the bee pattern on page 108. Instruct students to color their pattern, cut it out, and glue it to a wide craft stick. Then have them form two more pairs of legs and a pair of antennae from pipe cleaners to add to their puppet. Finally, invite students to buzz their bees around, using them to tell others about the characteristics that qualify the bee as a member of the insect family. You may want to review the parts of an insect (page 98).

★ BEE RESEARCHERS

Divide the class into small groups, then have each group do research to learn about bees. Students can use classroom and library books, Internet resources, and even personal interviews with local beekeepers as part of their research. If desired, write the questions below on chart paper and have students use them as a guide when searching for information about bees. After completing their research, encourage the group members to work collaboratively to compose a report of their findings. Then distribute photocopies of the stationery on page 109 for groups to use for their final drafts. Invite a volunteer from each group to share its report with the class. If desired, students can use their puppets from "Bee Puppet" (above) as part of their presentations.

- What is the role of a worker bee? A drone? A queen bee?

- How do bees communicate with each other?

- How do bees collect and transport nectar?

- How do honey bees convert nectar into honey?

- What role do bees play in flower pollination?

- Why and how is beeswax made?

LIFE CYCLE OF A BUTTERFLY

Beautiful butterflies develop from caterpillars by going through a process called metamorphosis. Distribute photocopies of pages 110–111 and have students cut out the wheel and picture wedges. Then, as you share the following information about the four stages of butterfly development with students, have them place the corresponding picture wedge on the appropriate section of the wheel:

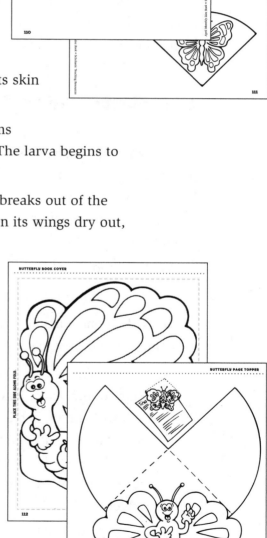

Stage 1: A female butterfly lays an egg on a leaf.

Stage 2: A caterpillar emerges from the egg. It eats the egg, then eats its home leaf and other surrounding leaves. The caterpillar, or larva, eats and eats, shedding its skin several times as it grows larger and matures.

Stage 3: The mature larva attaches to a branch and forms a hard case around itself. This case is called a chrysalis. The larva begins to change inside the chrysalis.

Stage 4: Once the larva's transformation is complete, it breaks out of the chrysalis. The new creature is hard to recognize, but when its wings dry out, the insect is easy to identify—it's a butterfly!

After students place all of the picture wedges in the correct sections on their wheel, have them glue the pieces in place. Then invite them to color the pictures.

 MORE ABOUT BUTTERFLIES

Encourage students to do additional research on butterflies, using the Internet, nonfiction books, and other sources. They might look up information to learn more about butterflies that migrate, how they gather food, how they protect themselves from predators, and so on. After students write the final draft of their findings, invite them to use page 112 to create a cover for their report. Or, have them color and cut out photocopies of the pattern on page 113 to create a page topper. To assemble, students simply fold the cutout back along the dashed lines, tape the straight edges together, and slip the butterfly over the top corner of their report.

★ BUTTERFLY CRAFTS

Complement your butterfly studies with these
fun-and-easy crafts.

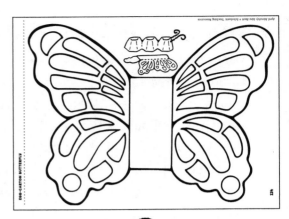

Egg-Carton Butterfly

Invite students to color and cut out the butterfly
pattern on page 114. Then have them glue a three-
cup section of an egg carton to the center of the
pattern. If desired, students can glue on
additional features, such as wiggle eyes and
pipe-cleaner antennae. After the glue dries,
help students fold the wings down to give
their butterfly a 3-D effect.

All A-Flutter Butterfly Mobile

These butterfly mobiles are fun to make and
display. To begin, distribute a photocopy of the butterfly
patterns (page 115) to each student, along with two 1-foot
lengths of yarn, scissors, a drinking straw, tape, and
craft items, such as glitter glue and sequins. Then have
students follow these directions to make a mobile:

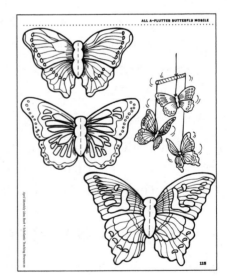

1. Color and cut out the patterns.

2. Fold each butterfly in half along the dashed lines.

3. Thread one length of yarn through the straw. Use
   tape to attach each end of the yarn to a butterfly.

4. Tie the other length of yarn snugly around the
   center of the straw, leaving the ends free. (Secure
   the yarn with tape to keep if from sliding
   along the straw.) Then tape the remaining
   butterfly to one loose end of the yarn. Tie a
   loop in the other end of the yarn to create a
   hanger.

5. Suspend the mobile from the ceiling,
   window frame, or a clothesline strung
   across the classroom.

Wonderful Wings Suncatchers

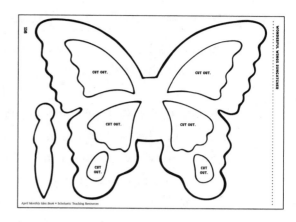

These butterfly suncatchers are perfect for a springtime window display. To prepare, distribute photocopies of the butterfly pattern on page 116, as well as scissors, scraps of colored tissue paper or cellophane, pipe cleaners, and glue (or clear tape). Then instruct students to do the following:

1. Color and cut out the butterfly body and wings. Then carefully cut out the six interior sections of the wings where indicated.

2. Glue the body to the center of the wings.

3. Choose six pieces of tissue paper or cellophane in the colors of your choice. Trim each piece to fit behind an opening in the wings. Glue (or tape) the pieces in place.

4. Form a pair of antennae from a length of pipe cleaner. Attach the antennae to your butterfly's head.

CREEPY CRAWLY CROSSWORD

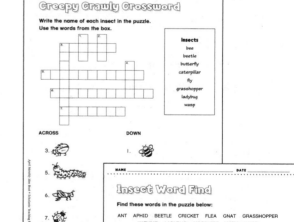

Give students practice with insect-related vocabulary and developing problem-solving skills with the crossword puzzle on page 117. Distribute photocopies to students, then demonstrate how to use the clues to find the answers and fill in the puzzle. Older students can work in pairs or small groups while you might work with younger students to help them complete the puzzle.

INSECT WORD FIND

Use the word find on page 118 to reinforce student's insect-related vocabulary. After students find and circle all of the insect names in the puzzle, have them complete the drawing activity at the bottom of the page.

LEARNING WITH LADYBUGS

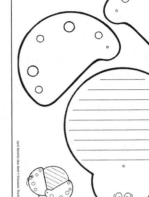

These hinged ladybugs make great center activities that can be used to reinforce a variety of skills. To assemble, cut out construction-paper copies of the ladybug and wing patterns on page 119. (Make as many copies as you need for the skill you plan to teach.) Program the two wings with the skill you want to teach and write the answer on the ladybug. Use a brass fastener to attach the pieces together, as shown. To use, students read the task, give their response, then separate the two wings to check their answer.

If desired, invite students to make their own hinged ladybugs. They might label the wings with a seasonal greeting (related to a ladybug or spring event) and write a special message on the ladybug. Or, they might write an insect-related riddle and its answer on the pieces.

THE HONEYBEE GAME

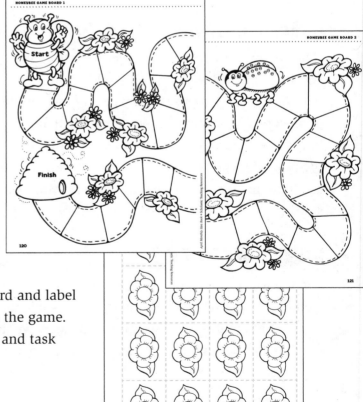

Use this game for a small-group or learning center activity. Or, make several copies of the game and divide the class into groups so they can all play at the same time! To get started, photocopy the game boards (pages 120–121). Glue the two parts of the game board together on poster board or to the inside of a file folder. How you use the game and what skills you want students to practice is up to you. Simply write the desired text (or problems) on the spaces of the game board and label a set of task cards (page 122) to use with the game. Then color and laminate the game board and task cards for durability.

Grasshopper Diagram

Label these insect parts:

Antennae   Abdomen   Head   Legs   Thorax   Wings

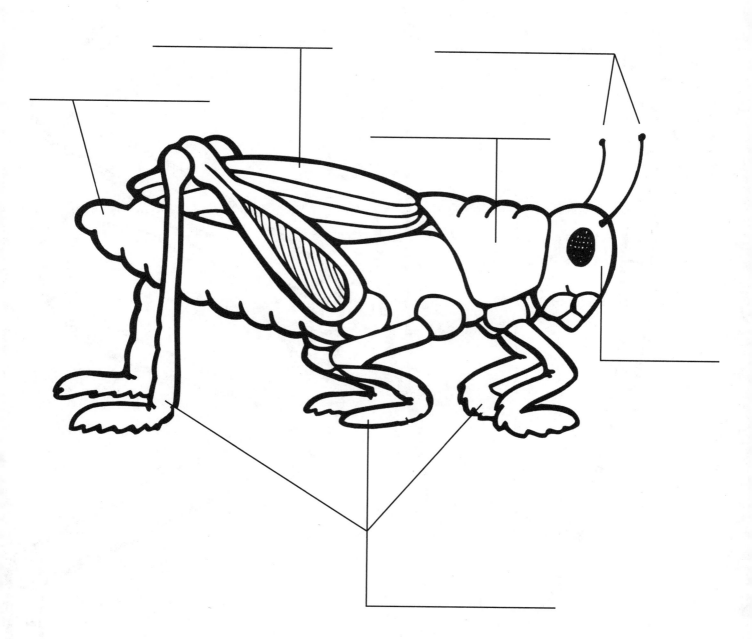

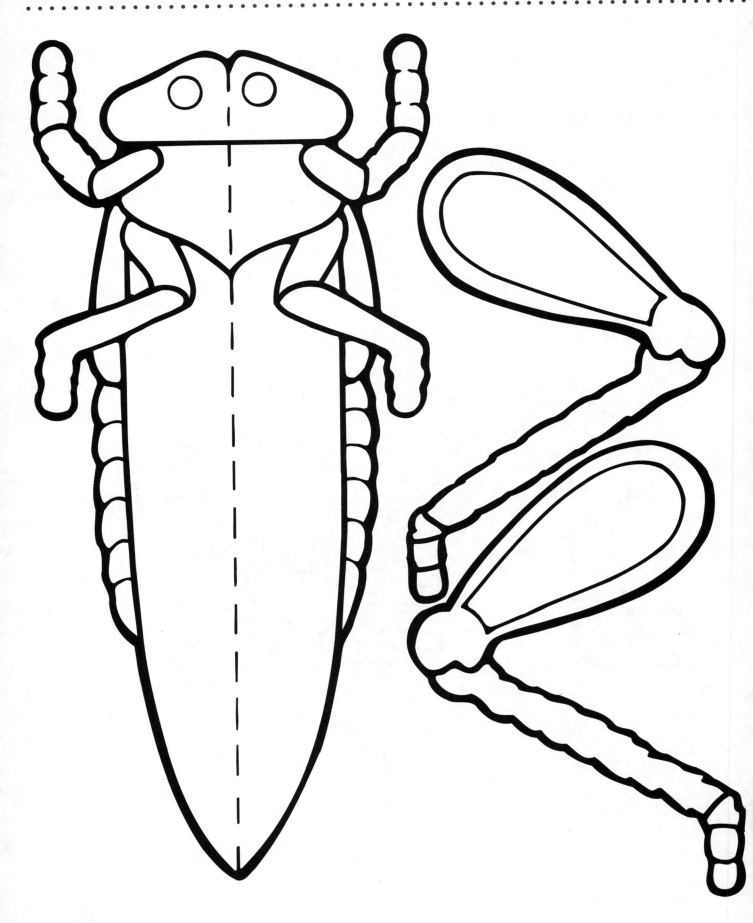

Interesting Insect!

My insect is _____

Here's a picture of my insect:

Facts about my insect:

Size: _____ Color(s): _____

Number of legs: _____ wings: _____ antennae: _____

My insect eats _____

It lives _____

It protects itself by _____

My insect lives about this long: _____

Another interesting fact about my insect: _____

_____

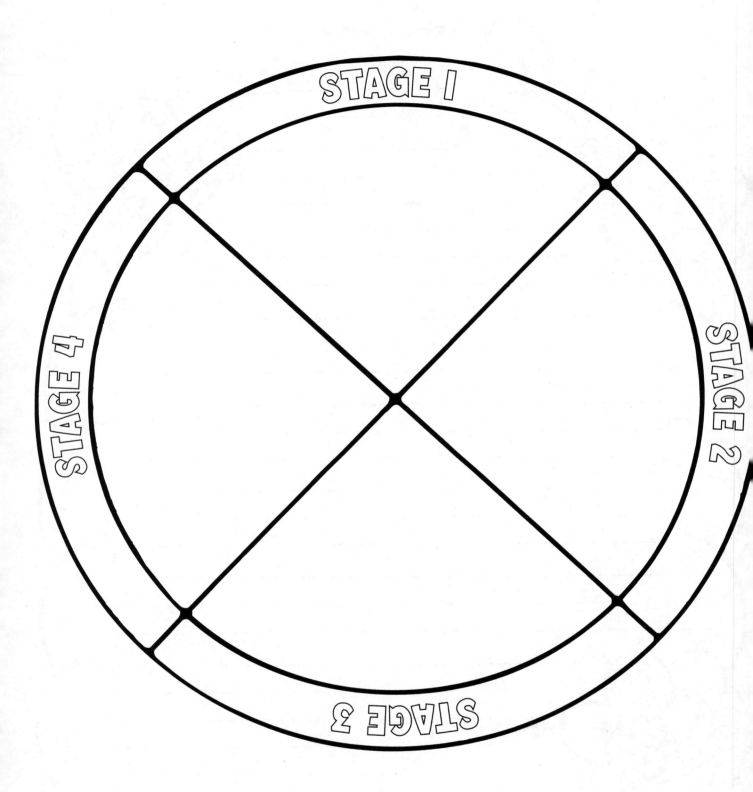

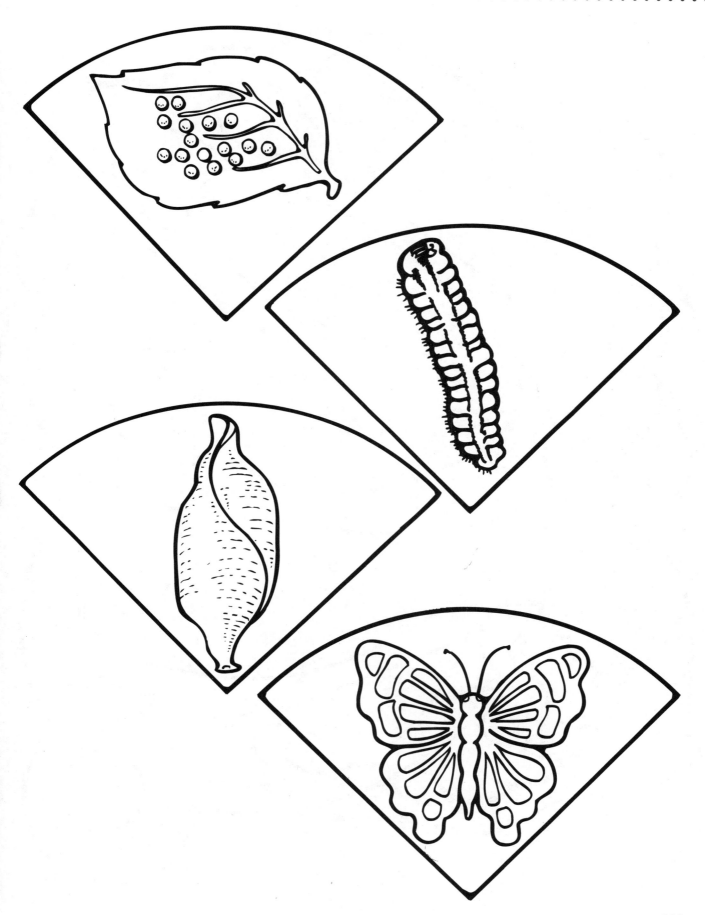

PLACE THIS SIDE ALONG FOLD.

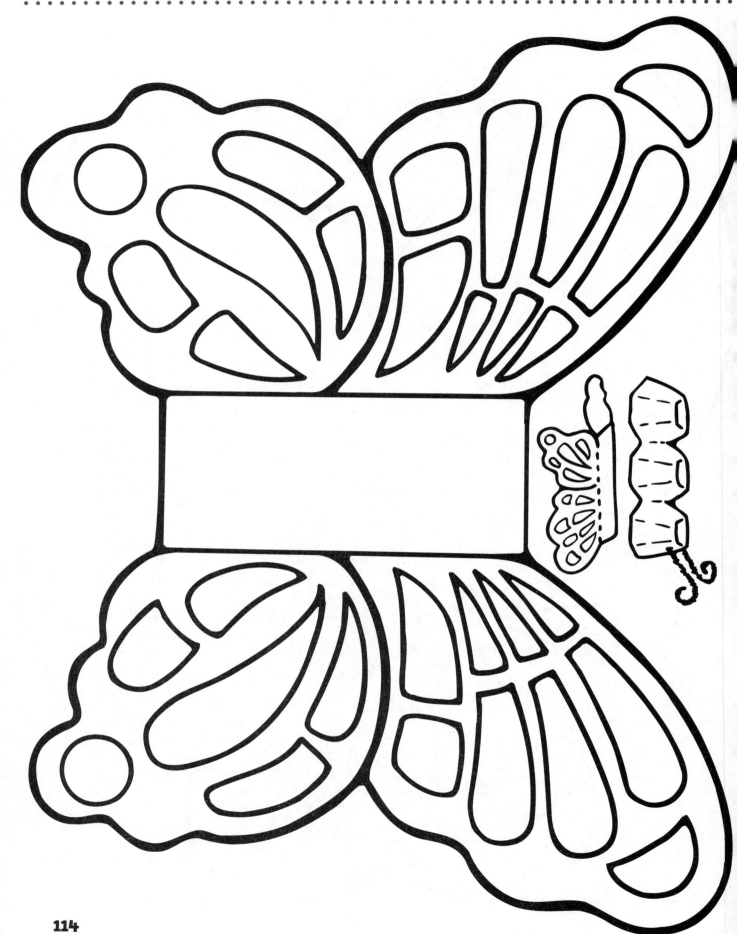

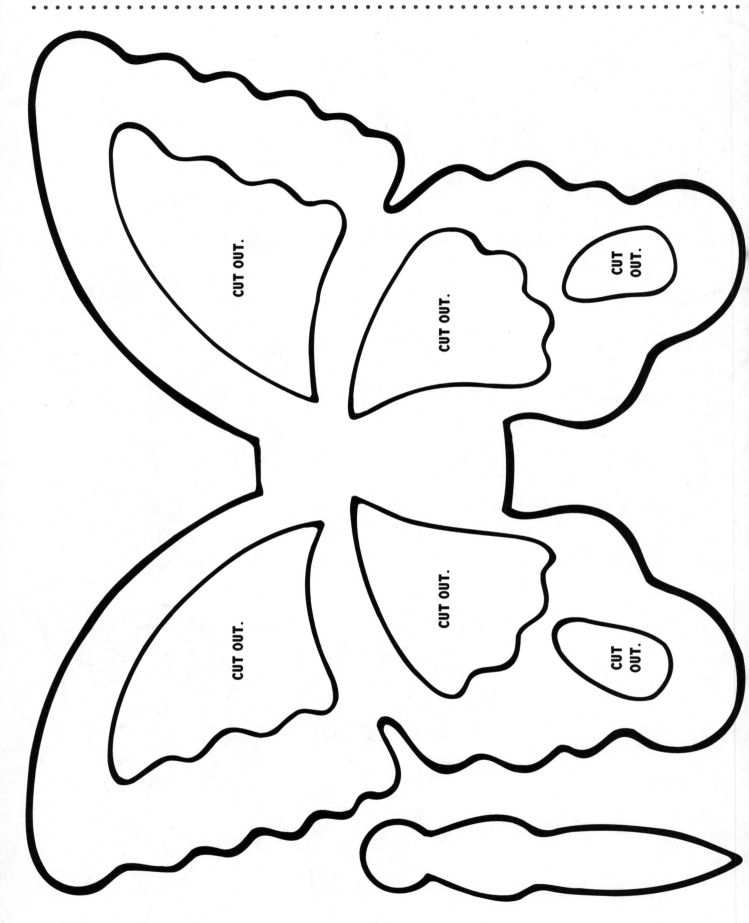

Creepy Crawly Crossword

Write the name of each insect in the puzzle.
Use the words from the box.

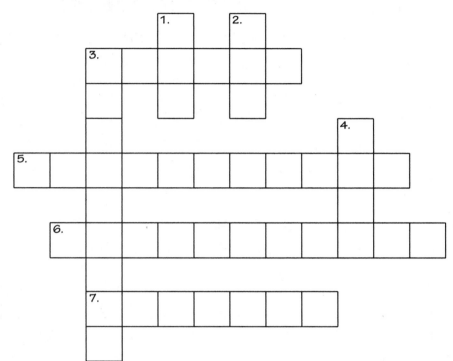

Insects

bee

beetle

butterfly

·

caterpillar

fly

grasshopper

ladybug

wasp

ACROSS

3.

5.

6.

7.

DOWN

1.

2.

3.

4.

Insect Word Find

Find these words in the puzzle below:

ANT   APHID   BEETLE   CRICKET   FLEA   GNAT   GRASSHOPPER
KATYDID   LADYBUG   MOSQUITO   MOTH   WASP

```
G N M K L O P L K M K N H G A S W E R T X
A L A D Y B U G F V K E S E D F T G H Y U
Z R I E I D S E D R A W U I C F T G B N B
Q E S D C R I C K E T Y F R C U S T O G N
A S E R A V B T H Y Y E W S C V F R G R J
A G N A T C O A D V D S F R B D E R T A Y
X L C O B F E N T I I T S W E C V B N S I
Q U X C E B G T D E D E E A L A S D M S U
A T D F E H X E R T Y M O S Q U I T O H E
Z R X C T G T F R E D F G P S D V B T O U
A Z F F L E A K F A R H E S T I M E H P T
W O S X E J P L O O N S C D R E T G H P N
M T D N A P H I D D E R T F G R D S W E R
A S D E R Q X C V J A Z U A T Y N H J R L
```

Choose two insects from the puzzle.

Draw them in the box.

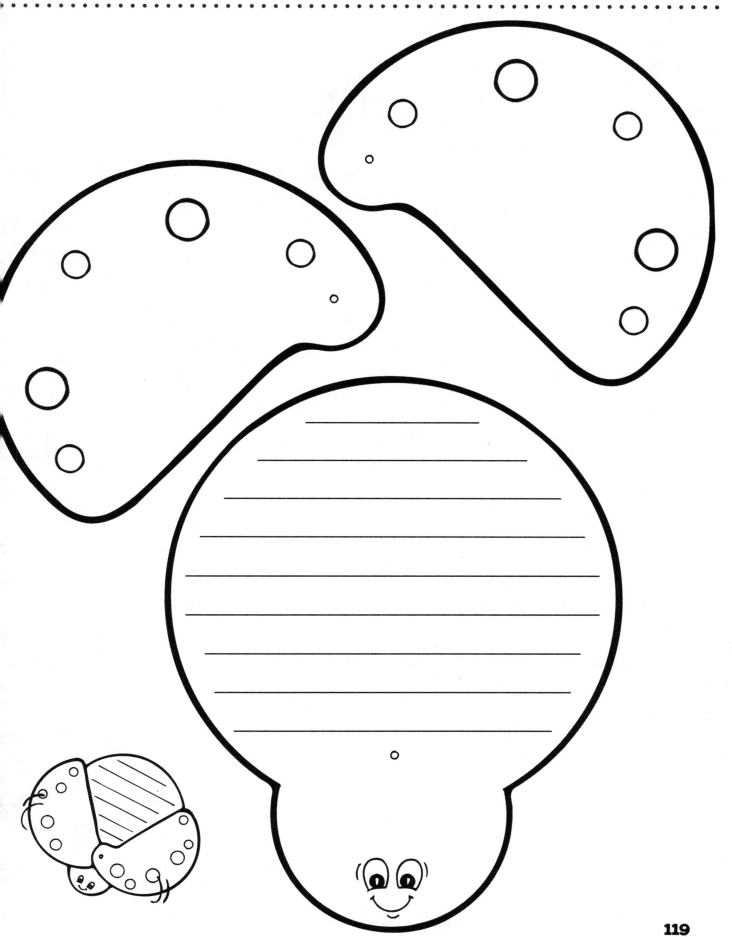

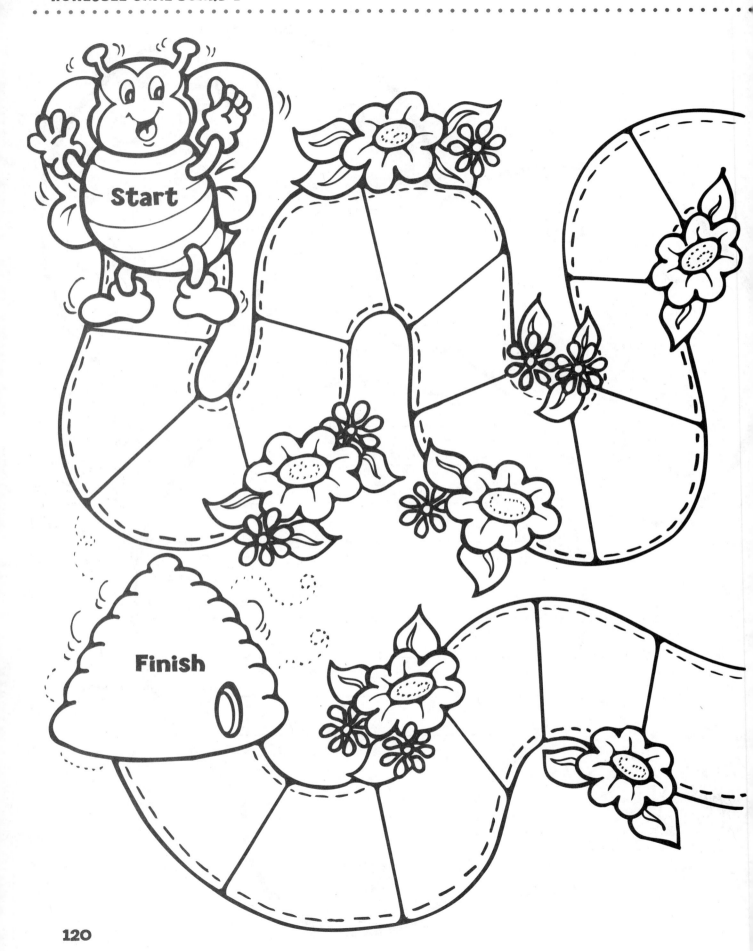

Start

Finish

OLYMPIC GAMES

The first known Olympic contest took place at the Stadium of Olympia in Ancient Greece in the year 776 B.C. The only contest at the early games was a footrace of about 200 yards. Later, events were added to include jumping, boxing, wrestling, and the javelin throw. Over time, the high standards and fair sportsmanship of the athletes declined. In the year 394 A.D. the Roman emperor Theodosius I abolished the games.

More than 1,500 years passed before the Olympic Games were revived. In 1892, a French baron named Pierre de Coubertin proposed bringing the competition back as a way to promote good will among countries around the world. He helped establish the International Olympic Committee (IOC), and on April 6, 1896, the Olympic Games were reborn. The first modern-day international competition was held in Athens, Greece with 280 participants from 13 nations competing in 43 events. Today, around 200 countries send athletes to participate in the Olympic Games, which are now regarded as the most prominent international sports competition.

Suggested Activities

★ TRADITIONAL DRESS PUPPETS

Divide the class into several groups. Explain that each group will research different aspects of Greek life and then present their findings to the class. Assign one topic (such as food, clothing, shelter, industry, art, or transportation) to each group to research. Students can use books available in the classroom as well as library books, Internet resources, and other sources such as videos and personal interviews for their research. Tell groups that they should look for information about life in Greece, both in the past and today, to compare how the people and culture have changed with the times. Younger students will enjoy hearing you read aloud from level-appropriate books on their topic. Afterward, they can discuss the information and then write and/or draw about what they have learned.

(continued)

Most groups will need a few days to complete their research for this assignment. To help students prepare their presentations, provide copies of the puppet patterns on pages 127–128 for them to cut out, color, and embellish with craft items. For example, a student might glue cloth to their puppets to represent traditional dress. They can glue wide craft sticks to their puppets to serve as handles. To extend the activity, have groups create posters to show what they've learned about their particular topic. Then invite students to use their puppets and posters to present their findings to the class.

★ GO-FOR-THE-GOLD WORD FIND

Distribute copies of the word find (page 129) to students and review the Olympics-related words listed on the page. After they find and circle the words in the puzzle, have students use some of these words to complete the writing assignment at the bottom of the page.

★ INTERNATIONAL SPORTS SYMBOLS

In today's Olympic Games, men and women from all over the world compete in more than 35 sports and over 400 different athletic events. To help athletes, volunteers, and observers cross the language barriers that naturally exist among people who speak different languages, symbols are often used to represent the various sporting events. Distribute photocopies of page 130 to students and review each symbol on the page. Talk about what sport each symbol might represent. If desired, copy the answers from page 143 in random order on chart paper. Then have students choose their answers from the list to complete the activity. Finally, instruct them to do the activity at the bottom of the page.

RESEARCHING OLYMPIC ATHLETES

Invite students to research and write about an Olympic champion whom they find interesting or inspiring. To begin, make a list of Olympic athletes from which students can choose their subject. (You might use the names below as well as any others that students are familiar with.) Then give each student a two-sided photocopy of the mini-book patterns (pages 131–132). Explain that students will use a variety of sources—such as library books, the Internet, and magazine articles—to research their chosen subject. After students complete their research, have them record their findings on their mini-book pages. To make the books, instruct students to do the following:

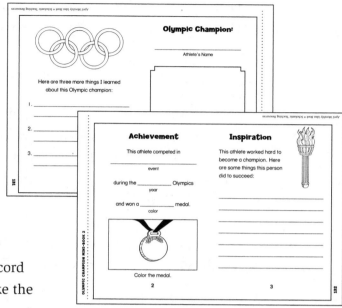

1. Fold the two-sided page in half, so that the cover is on the outside.

2. Fill in the athlete's name and draw his or her picture on the cover. Write your name on the author line.

3. Use your findings to fill in pages 2, 3, and 4.

4. If desired, add color and other embellishments, such as glitter and sports-themed stickers, to personalize your book.

Once students complete their mini-books, invite volunteers to share them with the class, along with other information they'd like to share about their Olympic champion.

Suggestions for Olympic Athletes

Kenenisa Bekele	Scott Hamilton	Edwin Moses	Wilma Rudolph
Usain Bolt	Yelena Isinbaeva	Apolo Ohno	Samuel Sanchez
Nadia Comaneci	Micki King	Jesse Owens	Frank Shorter
Kirsty Coventry	Olga Korbut	Anja Paerson	Keeth Smart
Janet Evans	Michelle Kwan	Michael Phelps	Picabo Street
Peggy Fleming	Carl Lewis	Mary Lou Retton	Zhang Yining

★ LAUREL HEAD WREATH

The ancient Greeks crowned Olympic champions with wreaths of laurel. Invite students to make their own laurel wreaths to wear whenever they meet a personal goal, complete a set of assignments, perform a task exceptionally well, or achieve any other notable accomplishment. To make their wreaths, distribute photocopies of page 131 to students. Have them color and cut out the patterns and then glue (or tape) the ends of the cutouts together to form a headband. (Some students may need to use more than two laurel patterns to make a headband that fits.)

★ MEDAL-WORTHY MOMENTS

Photocopy a supply of the medal patterns on page 134. Then, whenever students accomplish a goal, perform a random act of kindness, tackle a difficult task, participate in a challenge, or take part in a noteworthy activity, give them a copy of a medal to color with glitter crayons and then cut out. Help them cut an opening in the top of the medal where indicated. Then have students loop a length of yarn through the opening to make a necklace that they can wear around their neck.

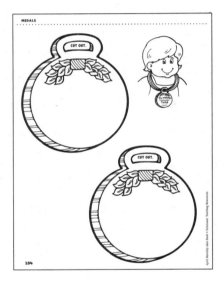

★ INSPIRATIONAL OLYMPIC WRITING

Distribute photocopies of page 135 for students to use in creative writing activities about the Olympic Games, Greek culture, sports, great athletes, or any other topic of their choice. They might write poems, skits, short stories, songs, or imaginary tales about their topic. When finished, invite volunteers to share their written work with the class.

Go-for-the-Gold Word Find

Find these words in the puzzle below:

ANTHEM   ATHLETE   BRONZE   BROTHERHOOD
CHAMPION   COMPETE   GOLD   MEDALS   PARTICIPANT
RELAY   SILVER   SPORTSMANSHIP   STADIUM   TORCH

```
G  N  M  K  L  G  O  L  D  M  K  N  H  G  A  S  W
A  S  Z  X  S  T  A  D  I  U  M  E  S  E  D  F  B
Q  R  I  O  N  D  S  E  S  R  A  W  U  I  C  F  R
Q  E  P  D  C  S  I  L  V  E  R  B  F  R  C  T  O
A  S  A  R  A  V  B  T  U  Y  Y  R  W  R  G  D  N
A  G  R  E  L  A  Y  A  S  V  D  O  C  R  M  D  Z
X  L  T  O  E  K  E  L  A  U  A  T  H  L  E  T  E
Q  U  I  C  O  M  P  E  T  E  D  H  A  A  D  A  L
A  T  C  F  T  H  A  E  R  T  Y  E  M  S  A  U  I
Z  R  I  C  O  G  L  F  R  X  D  R  P  P  L  D  N
A  S  P  O  R  T  S  M  A  N  S  H  I  P  S  U  S
W  O  A  X  C  J  P  L  O  O  N  O  O  D  R  E  T
M  A  N  T  H  E  M  I  D  D  E  O  N  F  G  R  D
A  S  T  E  R  Q  X  C  V  J  A  D  U  A  T  Y  N
```

Using six of the words from the puzzle, write a paragraph on what you enjoy about sports. If you need more space to write, use the back of this page.

_____

_____

_____

_____

International Sports Symbols

These symbols are often used to identify different Olympic sports.
Can you identify each sport? Write your answers on the lines below.

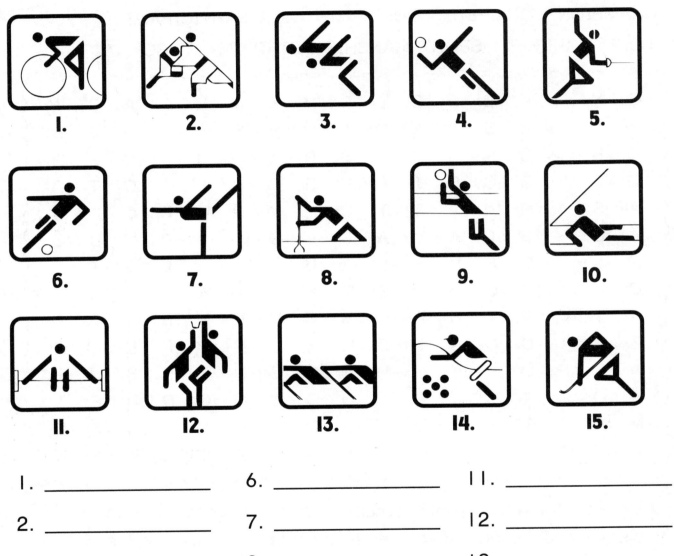

1.

2.

3.

4.

5.

6.

7.

8.

9.

10.

11.

12.

13.

14.

15.

1. _____   6. _____   11. _____

2. _____   7. _____   12. _____

3. _____   8. _____   13. _____

4. _____   9. _____   14. _____

5. _____   10. _____   15. _____

On the back of this page, draw a symbol to represent your favorite sport.

Olympic Champion:

Athlete's Name

Draw a picture of him or her.

by _____

Here are three more things I learned about this Olympic champion:

1. _____

2. _____

3. _____

4

Achievement

This athlete competed in

_____
event

during the _____ Olympics
year

and won a _____ medal.
color

Color the medal.

2

Inspiration

This athlete worked hard to become a champion. Here are some things this person did to succeed:

_____

_____

_____

_____

_____

_____

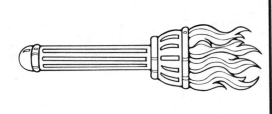

3

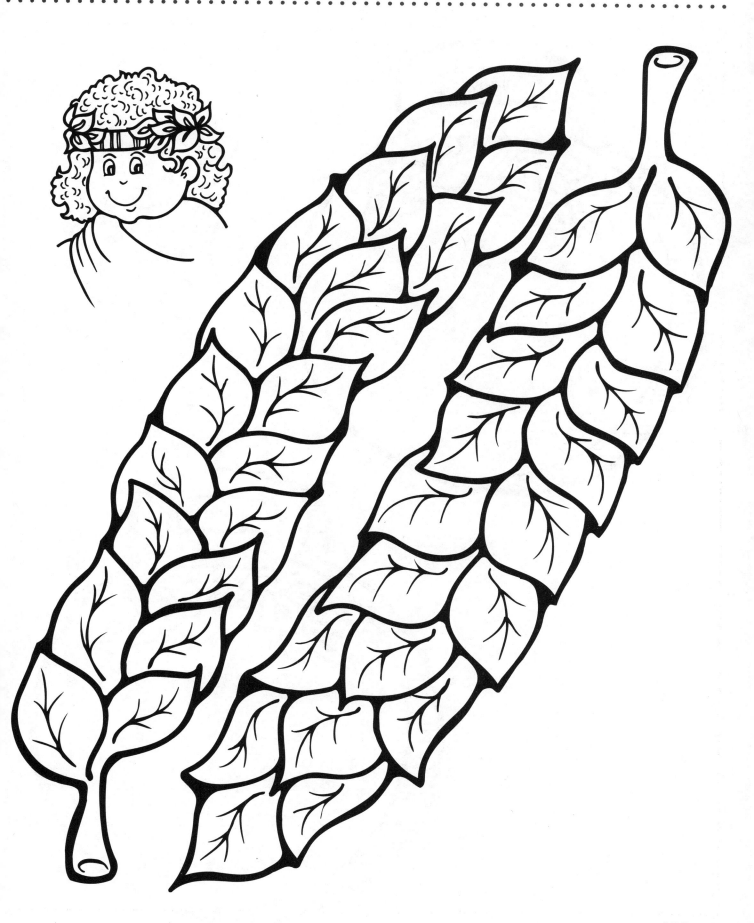

CUT OUT.

CUT OUT.

OLYMPIC
Todd

AWARDS, INCENTIVES, AND MORE

Getting Started

Make several photocopies of the reproducibles on pages 138 through 142. Giving out the bookmarks, pencil toppers, notes, and certificates will show students your enthusiasm for their efforts and achievements. Plus, bookmarks and pencil toppers are a fun treat for students celebrating birthdays.

- Provide materials for decorating, including markers, color pencils, and stickers.

- Encourage students to bring home their creations to share and celebrate with family members.

 ## BOOKMARKS

1. Photocopy onto tagboard and cut apart.

2. For more fanfare, punch a hole on one end and tie on a length of colorful ribbon or yarn.

 ## PENCIL TOPPERS

1. Photocopy onto tagboard and cut out.

2. Use an art knife to cut through the Xs.

3. Slide a pencil through the Xs as shown.

SEND-HOME NOTES

1. Photocopy and cut apart.

2. Record the child's name and the date.

3. Add your signature.

4. Add more details about the student's day on the back of the note.

 ## CERTIFICATES

1. Photocopy.

2. Record the child's name and other information, as directed.

3. Add details about the child's achievement (if applicable), then add your signature and the date.

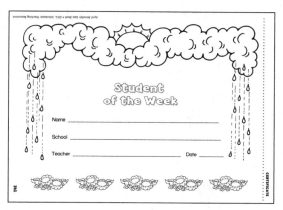

A book can be a good friend on a rainy day!

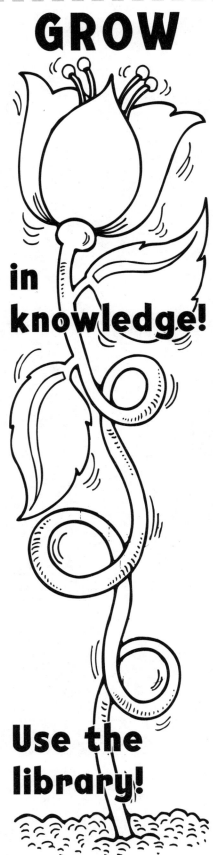

GROW

in knowledge!

Use the library!

"Bee"

a good reader!

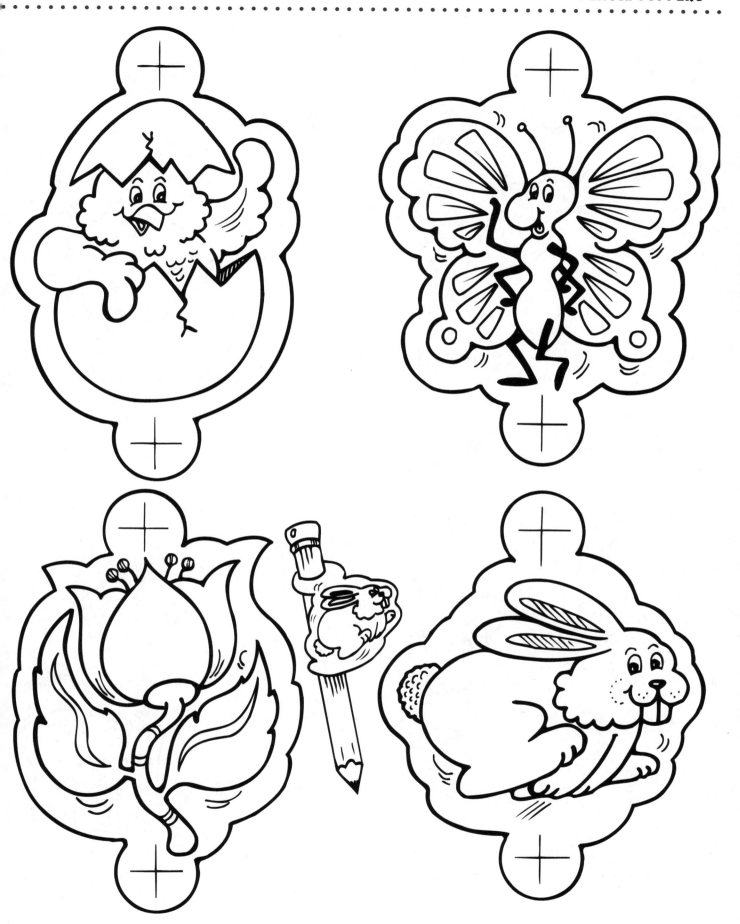

What a busy bee!

_____
Student's Name

did a great job today!

_____   _____
Date   Teacher

_____
Student's Name

did a super job today!

_____   _____
Date   Teacher

_____
Student's Name

was a joy in class today!

_____   _____
Date   Teacher

_____
Student's Name

worked hard today!

_____   _____
Date   Teacher

April Monthly Idea © 2012, Scholastic Teaching Resour

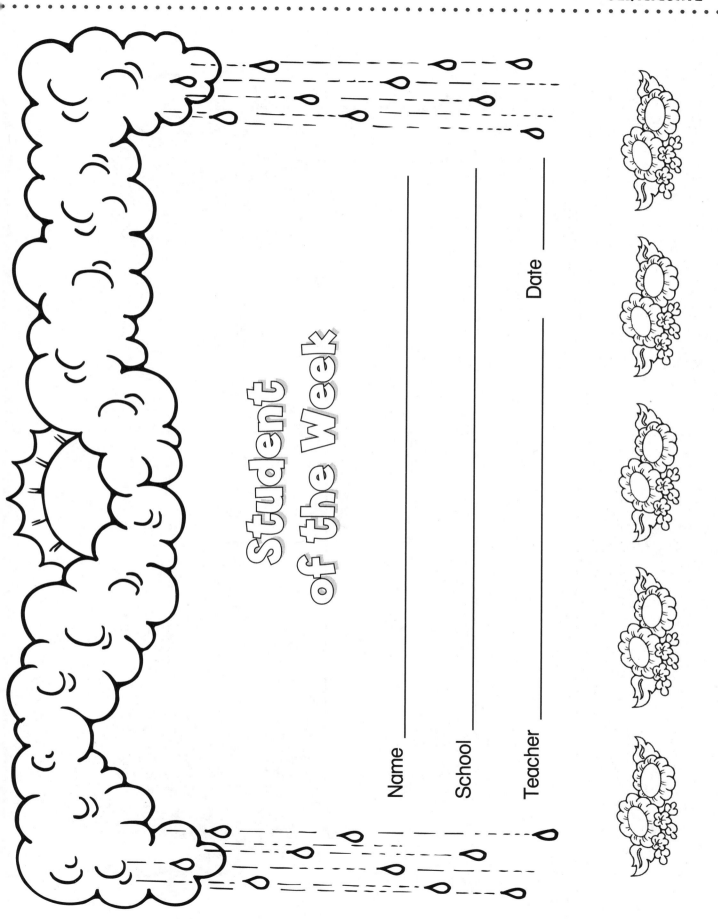

Student
of the Week

Name

School

Teacher

Date

Certificate of Achievement

Presented to

_____

Student's Name

in recognition of

_____

_____

Teacher

_____

Date

On-the-Nest Word Find, page 64

```
N R I C O G T F R X D Y P P S D N
F N M K L O P L A M K O H H O N W
O S Z X S T A D L U M L S A D E T
W R I O N P S E B E A K E T C S T
L P U L L E T C U E H B F C C T J
A C Z R A L B T M Y E R W H G D A
C H O C O L S H E L L O C R B D V
A I W O E E S L N U W I N G H T E
P C E M B R Y O D E D H A A E A L
O K C F T H E E R T C A P O N U I
```

Grasshopper Diagram, page 105

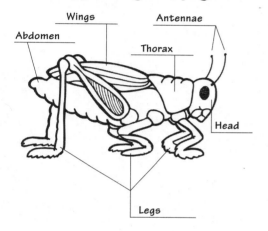

Wings

Antennae

Abdomen

Thorax

Head

Legs

Butterfly Life Cycle Wheel, page 110

STAGE 1

STAGE 2

STAGE 3

STAGE 4

Creepy Crawly Crossword, page 117

Insect Word Find, page 118

```
G N M K L O P L K M K N H G A S W E R T X
A L A D Y B U G F V K E S E D F T G H Y U
Z R I E I D S E D R A W U I C F T G H N L
Q E S D C R I C K E T Y F R C U S T O G N
A S E R A V B T H Y Y E W S C V F R G R J
A G N A T C O A D V D S F R B D E R T A Y
X L C O B F E N T I I T S W E C V B N S I
Q U X C E B G T D E D E E A L A S D M S U
A T D F E H X E R T Y M O S Q U I T O H O
Z R X C T G T F T G R F G P S D V B T H P
A Z F F L E A K F A R H E S T I M E H P E
W O S X E J P L O O N S C D R E T G H P N
M T D N A P H I D D E R T F G R D S W R R
A S D E R Q X C V J A Z U A T Y N H J R L
```

Choose two insects from the puzzle.

Go-for-the-Gold Word Find, page 129

```
G N M K L G O L D M K N H G A S W
A S Z X S T A D I U M E S E D F B
Q R I O N D S E S R A W U I C F R
Q E P D C S I L V E R B F R C T O
A S A R A V B T U Y Y R W R G D N
A G R E L A Y A S V D O C R M Z
X L T O E K E L A U A T H L E T E
Q U I C O M P E T E D H A A D A L
A T C T H A E R T Y M A S A U I
Z R I C O G L F R X D R P A L D N
A S S P O R T S M A N S H I P S T
W O A X C J P L O O N O D R E T
M A N T H E M I D D E O N F G R D
A S T E R Q X C V J A D U A T Y N
```

International Sports Symbols, page 130

1. Cycling
2. Judo
3. Swimming
4. Handball
5. Fencing
6. Football /Soccer
7. Gymnastics
8. Canoeing
9. Volleyball
10. Yachting
11. Weightlifting
12. Basketball
13. Rowing
14. Pentathlon
15. Hockey